C000255528

To Toby

TRUE RED

Tuhoe show

Best Wishes

22 / 2 / 2016

Tuhoe 'Bruno' Isaac with Bradford Haami
True Red©℗2007

Warning: This book contains graphic violence and offensive language
that may offend some readers.

First published in 2007 by:
True Red
P. O. Box 1362, Pukekohe, New Zealand.
Email Sales: brunotuhoeisaac@gmail.com

ISBN 978-0-473-12843-2

Copyright©2009 Tuhoe Isaac

All rights reserved. No part of this publication may be reproduced, stored in a
retrieval system, or transmitted in any form or by any means, electronic, mechanical,
including photocopying, recording otherwise, without prior permission of the publisher.
National Library of New Zealand cataloguing-in-Publication Data.

Design by Billy McQueen and Bradford Haami, photography by Fraser Clements,
2nd reader Michelle Shannon, edited and proof-read by Grant Webby.
Front cover photo: Tuhoe Isaac 2007. Inside cover photo: Tuhoe's contemplation.
Back cover photo: Tuhoe's tattooed patch on his back. Back inside cover photo:
A portrait image of Tuhoe, 2007. (All photographs taken by Fraser Clements).
Bible scriptures taken from The NIV Topical Study Bible, New International
Version, 1989, The Zondervan Corporation.

Printed and bound in New Zealand.

For comments and further information go to www.true-red.com.

CONTENTS

GLOSSARY

Aotearoa	New Zealand
Aroha	sadness, love
Block	pack rape
Boob	slang for prison
Boob head	inmate
Boob glove	tattoos on the fist and fingers
Hakihaki	sores
Handle	nickname
Hapu	pregnant, sub-tribe
Hei aha!	So what!
Hoha	nuisance, pest
Hongi	greeting by pressing noses
Hourangi	drunk
Iwi	tribe
Kai	food
Kai moana	sea food
Kapahaka	traditional dance troupe
Kaumatua	elders
Kaupapa	strategy, subject
Kiore	rat
Koha	donation
Kuia	old woman
Kumara	sweet potato
Lag	prison term
Mana	power, authority
Manuhiri	visitors

Maori	indigenous people of New Zealand
Marae	tribal gathering place
Moko	facial tattoo
Paipera tapu	Holy Bible
Pakeha	non-Maori
Papakainga	original home
Paua	abalone shellfish and shell
Patch	gang emblem sewn on to the back of leather jacket vest
Pawhara	split open to dry
Poroporoaki	farewell ceremony
Rakiraki	ducks
Redemption	take the rap/pay the price
Reggies	layers of jeans sewn together and never washed
Reo	Maori language
Ruru	night owl
Screw	prison warden
Tag	nickname
Tangihanga	three day mourning ceremony for a dead person
Tapu	levels of sacredness
Tikanga	tribal protocols
Tupapaku	dead corpse
Utu	revenge, reciprocal payment or action
Whakapapa	genealogy
Whanau	family
Whanaungatanga	friendly relationships
Whare	house

ACKNOWLEDGEMENTS

I would like to thank all those who supported this kaupapa and contributed to this project's fruition with your advice, comments, encouragement, investment, time and expertise. Special thanks to the New Zealand Herald, Franklin News and Arno for permission to publish photographs.

Arohanui atu.

Tuhoe.

DEDICATION

I dedicate this book to the memory of my parents
Jim and Ngahuia Isaac.

FOREWORD

Listening to ex-Mongrel Mob leader Tuhoe 'Bruno' Isaac speak at a seminar in 2006 I was reminded of my own childhood days in the mid-1970s where gangs were a pervasive part of our rural Aotearoa/ New Zealand communities. As Tuhoe spoke, many questions leapt into my mind. Why the dog and the Nazi swastika? How is it that brothers and cousins in rival gangs could fight and kill each other? What led him to leave the gang lifestyle? When did Tuhoe finally recognise that his execrable life wasn't, in its essence, really who he was? After a brief discussion with Tuhoe that day, we came to an arrangement to intersect with these questions and to write his story in a published form. He had been approached before but none of those offers flew.

After a series of in-depth discussions with Tuhoe, and others from his past, it quickly became apparent to me how ignorant we are - and I include myself in this - of gang life in Aotearoa/New Zealand. Most of our knowledge of gangs is so linked to what is portrayed in the media headlines and talkback shows rather than confronting the subject with a cold eye. Tuhoe and people like him have never had a platform to be heard except from the courtroom dock or the court pages of the newspapers. Let's face it: the Mongrel Mob is so alienated from the day-to-day roundabout of our everyday lives that most would never give these guys the time of day. However, with the rising tide of gang-related violent crime in Aotearoa/

New Zealand today, there is a swell of interest in trying to understand the gang consciousness in a bid to unearth some answers.

It was not an easy process for Tuhoe to relive his dark past. The more he opened up to me - delving into a past he'd all but forgotten - the more we recognised incidents and themes that resurrected themselves time and time again throughout his life. These themes and events lingered and impacted in Tuhoe's life journey dragging him into a swamp of gang life that almost led to his death. The point at which he knew he had to break the cycle of lawlessness, sexual perversity and violence became as defining as St Paul's road to Damascus experience, poised as Tuhoe was at a crossroads between a society clamoring for answers to a gang lifestyle that had him in an octopus grip, and a new awakening.

It is not my wish to glorify Tuhoe's past gang exploits but to nakedly unravel the reality of his life inside the 'house of the dog', to present the life of someone who has been released from the parched landscape of alienation. Understanding how he could achieve personal change took Tuhoe years of soul-searching and it still remains an abiding pilgrimage. Change is the central theme of this book and it is this part of his life I was most interested in writing about - what did it really take for someone like Tuhoe, consumed by unadulterated mongrelism, to leave that existence and readjust his entire mindset? Most of us do not have the wherewithal to leap out of the boxes we call our lives and to confront our deepest flaws, hidden secrets, raw emotions and hurts and reflect on the consequences of our past actions; to step away from those parts of our lives that are not only destructive to ourselves but to all those around us. Tuhoe faced his personal demons and made a courageous choice to become new. This is a life story of raw courage, insight, doggedness and sheer bloody-mindedness in a transformation against the great odds of sexual molestation, brutalising criticism, incarceration, drug and alcohol abuse, duplicity, crippling loneliness and isolation.

True Red gets under the skin of aspects of Aotearoa New Zealand society seldom understood or penetrated. It is also a true story of hope and redemption for the next generation who wrestle with the same darkness, disenfranchisement and lawlessness Tuhoe lived with. He is a fearless example of how one can rise out of the ashes of personal corruption and begin a momentum from the profane to the sacred.

I am privileged to have had the opportunity to sit with Tuhoe and unreservedly ask strong questions about his past, present and future so the reader of this book may truly understand the plight of those who have lived, and still live this experience. This journey has given me more compassion, understanding and love for those people whom society considers unlovable and unknowable. I applaud the mammoth soul-searching task required to change your life Tuhoe. Kia kaha, kia maia, kia manawanui. Arohanui, Tukua to korero kia rere. Na to hoa,

Na Bradford Haami,
Tamaki-makau-rau, September 2007.

INTRODUCTION

In the public's mind the Mongrel Mob have a notorious reputation as an unpredictable and dangerous gang. We were thought of as Maori gangsters whose lives revolved around fear, violence, drugs, drinking, brawling, rape and murder. I do not dispute this public image but from an insider's point of view the Mongrel Mob gave me a total sense of belonging at a crucial time in my life. Here I found true acceptance and comradeship amongst a common brotherhood; I was willing to die for them. The Mob became everything to me: it was my life and it was also to be my death. Or so I believed. Living in this zone allowed me to embrace a rebellious life that was spawned out of neglect, abuse, poverty and loneliness. It satisfied my desire for violence, lust, seduction and anything else I desired to feed my distorted ego. Gang life allowed me to stand up and fight against a society that hated us. For seventeen years I lived in the 'house of the dog' where my mind, body and spirit were totally entrenched in the mentality of mongrelism. To change that mindset would have taken nothing short of a miracle. I was true red; I conformed to the gang's colours and was totally ensconced into the world of the dog.

There was a time in my gang life where I thought I was physically dying. My mentality at that time was 'Seig Heil Dog' in the sense that life was meaningless, if I die I die, hei aha! Who cares? It must be time for me to go to the mighty bulldog in the sky. But deep inside me, even though I was unconscious of it at the time, I wanted to live, I wanted to change but I had no idea what that meant or how to achieve it. It was to take me years to dig myself out of a hole, to walk out of the 'house of the dog'.

Coming out of the gang was a lonely journey. Stepping outside the safety of the Mongrel Mob haven I felt the judgmental eyes of the public crawl like maggots all over my body. The stereotypes and prejudices people had about gang members and being Maori to boot - that we can never be transformed - reared its ugly head and could easily have become a deterrent to my desire for change. I was constantly bombarded with the sense that society was never going to accept someone like me anyway. Mainstream society was a very lonely place filled with rejection and distrust. I know, I've been there.

Living outside of the Mob is probably the hardest thing I have had to experience in my whole life; it's challenges, confrontations and reconciliations have changed the way I view life. I've had to lay my life out naked and stare at a past devoid of any sense of morality. Coming to the realisation I'd inflicted pain on others pushed me to a psychological crossroads, and I was propelled down a road foreign to the culture of the Mob to the path of open confession and seeking forgiveness.

I have tripped up, been friendless and lonely, battered by a self-condemnation that tore at my soul, saved from hatred and death, fed when I was starving and rebuked when I've felt the pull of the dog return like iron filings caught in the field of a magnet. It was a journey through fire and the heat came close to suffocation. But I survived.

When I decided to commit my memoirs to paper I called a meeting with a number of ex-Mongrel Mob members, now out of 'the house of dog,' to discuss the idea. I stood before those brothers and asked forgiveness if there was anything in my past gang life that hurt or offended them. We shook hands and forgave each other for our pasts and laughed about the times we'd tried to take each other out in a blaze of gunfire. They agreed our stories needed to be told for the sake of our brothers, sisters, wives and most of all our children, who need to learn from our mistakes: there is another way other than the life we chose.

This manuscript will give the public of Aotearoa/New Zealand a glimpse into the plight of the unwashed, the underprivileged, the unloved, the lost, the fatherless, the disinherited, the rejected, the disenfranchised, the poverty stricken and the uneducated. Those unfortunate enough to have been born in to these ghettos gravitate easily to the gang world. For those who struggle with violence, gangs, prisons, loneliness and the mentality of despair I have only one point to make: there is life after the gangs. For the last fifteen years I have been on a journey that faced up to and dealt with the consequences of my past. I had to take responsibility and own up to my own actions. Overcoming my past has enabled me to face a future removed from captivity and with my awakened conscience intact. My mission is to convey a message to those still chained to a gang life - new life is possible but you have to want it. I hope an insight into my life may offer thoughts and possible solutions for the growing youth gang phenomenon.

I make no apology for the raw and sometimes shocking nature of this story, to tell it any differently would be to dilute the truth. This book begins with an insight into my past Mongrel Mob mindset. It is followed by a commentary on my upbringing and the journey to young adulthood when I entered the gang. After traversing my gang experience the book concludes with my struggle to find a new pathway for life. My family and children's names have not been identified here for personal and safety reasons. Known nicknames or aliases have been used to protect the real identity of those mentioned in the story. Writing this book may open old wounds and draw out old enemies but beyond that I know that many people who knew me in the past will be able to relate to what I am about to share. Ultimately, the aim is not to put my own name up on a pedestal - but more to show how a violent, evil-hearted gangster can be pulled out of darkness into the world of light. Anei taku tahuhu korero: Here is my life story.

Tuhoe 'Bruno' Isaac.
Pukekohe, 2007.

TRUE RED

The life of an ex-Mongrel Mob Gang Leader

Tuhoe 'Bruno' Isaac with Bradford Haami

True Red

Chapter One
THE DOG RULES

For seventeen years the Mongrel Mob gang was the centre of my life and the ethos of the dog ruled every facet of existence. The image of the bulldog wearing a 'Krautlid' - the German Stahlhelm helmet exhibiting a swastika - was the gang emblem I wore on my back and had tattooed all over my body. It symbolised the mongrel dog spirit and was, to put it quite simply, an emblem that screamed anti-society. 'Seig Fucken Heil' was our rally cry. Many have asked why the British bulldog stood as our gang symbol. The bulldog was a symbol of the British colonial oppression that consumed the Maori people. The guys figured if you put that image on a Maori's back, with the dog wearing a German helmet with a swastika attached to it, then you had a dual symbol of contradiction and hatred. That is what we stood for - that was who I was.

We felt all levels of society - our fathers and mothers, whanau, Pakeha, Maori, neighbours, towns, churches, politicians and the public - hated us, so we just reflected that hatred back at them like a high-noon sun in a mirror. The swastika symbol, taken on board by the original gang members, stood for the enemies our fathers and grandfathers fought against and detested in World War II. In our perversity we appropriated that symbol, proclaimed it as our own and set ourselves up as public enemy number one. Red was our colour and it stood for blood, the blood spilt by our brothers and the blood we shed as a gang.

We created a new society based on hatred, a transformation embodied in the symbol of the dog. We took on the habits of the bulldog - its ferocity, fearlessness and growling persona; its barking language, its territorial nature and its feeding and sexual habits. The dog's features were engraved on our hearts and souls and this became manifest in our actions.

It is intriguing how the name Mongrel Mob was coined. The origins of the gang title, as we heard it, came from some guys from the East Coast of New Zealand who were in court on criminal charges. In the judge's summing-up he made a statement describing the accused as a 'pack of mongrels'. From that point on the term Mongrel Mob stuck like congealed blood and was taken on board as our name.

In my era there were no rules except the 'law of lawlessness.' If it was considered evil, bad and lawless we embraced it as good; everything was backwards or ironic. The 'mystery' of the gang was that we were right even if we were wrong; we were good even if we were bad. We embraced a living contradiction. The Mob psyche may have made no sense to outsiders but everything we did made perfect sense to us. Being a Mongrel meant being able to do anything your mind could conceive; any form of fantasy or debauchery you were able to dream up was acceptable.

If you weren't a Mobster you weren't worth knowing. We treated the rest of the world as if they didn't exist. Those outside our orbit were to be used and abused for our own ends. Women were there to cook our kai and give us pleasure - they were simply chattels, meat we could consume and spit out. Everything was on tap: drugs, alcohol, sex, violence and even death. Taking the 'bash' meant you were one of the bros and to 'get the bash' was our way of showing love to our brothers and sisters. The gang pad became a convening place where the like-minded could gather.

The gang patch worn on our backs was a mark of acceptance into the brotherhood of the Mob. Possessing it meant you had proved yourself a member worthy to wear the symbol of mongrelism, the dog, and all the hatred that went with it. The prerequisite for obtaining a patch meant taking on a lag as a prospect where you did whatever you were told to do, from cleaning floors and robbery to fighting, together with a grab-bag of anti-social behaviour and crime. Some of this was disgusting to say the least. A meeting would be called and if the president and the fellow gang members felt you cut the mustard you were in. Receiving your patch was a sign of your commitment to the cause of the dog. You would defend your gang patch to the death. It was more important than anything, it was more important than your wife, kids, family and friends, and without it you were nothing. It was the pinnacle of success and signified an allegiance to the Mob that overrode any other form of relationship.

Associated with the patch was being christened with a new name. We were all given a nickname, customarily derived from an incident in your life or an aspect of your nature. Real names were never used and aliases were common.

Brawls and rumbles were part of our daily diet and that often meant fighting against our own brothers and cousins who were in rival gangs. All family ties were severed when you joined the Mob and many people have struggled to comprehend this. It was pretty simple really - being a patched member of the Mongrel Mob meant that from that point on your first allegiance was to the gang brotherhood. All connections to family - parents, brothers, sisters, cousins and friends - didn't matter whatsoever. All relationships from our pasts just evaporated. Those of our blood families in rival gangs were just as much enemies as their peers we had no connection with. However, in saying that, some Mob members who respected their families and held on to those relationships would visit their family homes in a clean and well-dressed manner, but the minute they stepped out the door they would change back into their Mob gears in allegiance to the way of the dog.

The hierarchical system in the gang meant you started as a prospect and moved on to become a patched member. Life as a prospect could be a long time and you had to do the bidding of your overseer and execute whatever he told you to do. This could mean carrying out all the dirty tasks, cleaning and cooking as well as being forced to immerse yourself in cruel and disgusting acts. Sometimes this meant performing a crime that would send you to prison to do your time among other hardened brothers. They then judged whether you had the stomach to wear the Mongrel Mob patch on your back or not. Prospects were our slaves in the line of duty until we decided they had transitioned from that status to fully patched member. Drinking excrement and urine from a gumboot, raping someone, or fighting three guys at once for one minute and surviving on your feet showed your dedication to the dog. These degrading acts desensitised you to any form of intimidation or brutality your enemies, your brothers and society, could throw at you. After this a prospect might receive his patch. Being patched was the proudest day in the life of a prospect and was the apex of existence. You were finally recognised as one of the Mongrel

Mob. Some of the young guys often found the lifestyle and the daily tasks of a prospect hard and relentless and they would run away. But there was no escape from the Mob; prospects that absconded were always forcibly returned and severely bashed for their disobedience. Some guys were prospects for years.

Holding on to the patch for dear life was paramount. If you lost it - either figuratively or literally - you were considered nothing. It was a very hard to retrieve it back or to receive that blessing again from your own chapter. Wearing a patch meant supporting the actions of the gang. If you didn't support the entire Mob spirit then you may as well get out. If you were outwardly seen as unsupportive of your brothers in a crime or you performed some act against the Mob you could be de-patched and the retribution was savage. If you ran away from a fight wearing your patch you were classed as a coward and you'd be de-patched and probably cop a beating. You were a marked man throughout the whole country. Wearing a chapter patch came with a lot of responsibility. You had to live up to what and who you said you were, and that meant not being intimidated by the law, and trusting only the bulldog inside of you and no one else. Literally losing your patch or being de-patched for anti-mongrel behaviour meant you were now less than a dog, you were possibly now human.

The president sat at the top, followed in order by the vice-president, the sergeant-of-arms, the treasurer, patched members and the prospects. The president made the major decisions for the particular gang chapters. He was the one we regarded as our main role model for life; he was our life blood and we looked up to everything he did; he was our protection and encouraged us to fight on and stay staunch when the odds looked bad. To back all this up he had to be physically strong, courageous and able to defend himself. His loyalty to the brotherhood was uncompromising and he often took the rap for others' crimes. Attributes such as harshness and violence were accepted along with fairness and charity. The art of being able to rip off anyone outside the Mob was also another trait of the leaders. Loyalty to the brotherhood was perhaps the most important quality for a leader coupled with the maintenance of the 'mana' or power of the Mob. Mana in our eyes was gained through wickedness, evil and fear; this was the backbone of mongrelism. The power of your reputation was what moved you up the ranks. 'Meanest is the greatest' secured your position within the gang and this was never truer than with the presidents. They were role models and captains of our lives, above the rule of kings and queens, princes and princesses, politicians and police, kaumatua and fathers. I idolised them; everything they were I wanted to be. If your president had a mohawk haircut we all had a mohawk; if he was happy we were all happy; if he was mad we were all mad. When they died their words echoed in our heads for years afterwards; they were our idols. The hung framed photos of dead presidents memorialised and cemented the love we had for them and the authority they had over our lives.

Comradeship was central to our lives, and whatever was decided for the good of the brotherhood everyone agreed to. We believed in 'one for all and all for one'. Notions of being 'staunch' and 'macho' and not taking any 'crap' from anyone meant we used fear as a major weapon to manipulate any situation to our advantage. The mongrel in me growled: 'Don't mess with me, don't look at me and never bow down to anyone.' An emotionless face, a snarl on the lips, an intimidating walking style - the boob shuffle - and an attitude that looked down our noses at those who weren't part of the brotherhood was how we projected ourselves to the general public. The only emotions unsuppressed in us were anger and hatred. Love did not exist. This was also the public's view of us. Those who were not part of us were considered weak 'sissy' wimps and not worth the time of day. Accepting acts of kindness and general courtesies from society meant nothing to us, we saw them as signs of weakness. We compounded this attitude with uncleanliness. As far as we were concerned Mongrel Mob attitudes superceded every other form of social, political or religious ethic.

Being good meant the loss of power and authority in the ethos of the Mongrel Mob. For instance, I remember hiding the fact that someone had given me a Bible or even a book as it made me look weak in the eyes of my comrades. You couldn't afford to accept anything the Mob could view as foreign or good, lest your reputation became tarnished as a traitor. Crucially, there was always someone within the ranks who would look at any sign of weakness as an opportunity to challenge your position within the gang; you had to keep the mask of the mongrel not only on your face minute-by-minute but deep in your heart if you were to survive at all.

Alcohol and drugs for many of us was a bonding agent. We inhabited the pubs, playing our own sounds there, and the bars became so much a part of our territory that no-one else had the right to enter without our consent. Often we walked in broke and walked out rich and drunk. Booze was the super-glue that sealed all our relationships.

Being Maori meant nothing to us even though the majority of us were Maori; the only culture worth anything to us was Mob culture. The patch replaced all ethnic or cultural dimensions. You never spoke the reo (Maori language), or performed a hongi (greeting by pressing noses) within the confines of the gang or the gang pad in my time. All that 'Maori stuff' was to be left on the marae or wherever it was normally lived out. 'Don't bring that crap to the pad,' we would say. I never ever identified myself as being Maori while I was in the Mob - why would I? My culture was not recognised or even accepted by the dog. Dog culture was the ruling power in my life.

My language as a Mobster was like the barking, snarling, howling and growling of a dog and only a true mongrel could understand it. We had our own slang, full of swearing, with every third or fourth word in a sentence omitted. Even the voice modulation - the changing tones, various volume levels and slurs - had special meanings for us. Everyone had their own dog snarl - it was a separate language of its own, the language of the dog.

There was nothing hidden or sacred about our lives. Everyone knew you intimately - living together, eating together, fighting together, dying together - every aspect of your life was transparent among the tight circle of brothers. There were no secrets. We robbed banks, raped and committed crimes without masks. There was no shame in committing crimes, that's who we were and we were proud of it. Being fearless, being stabbed or shot at, continually fighting, or taking the rap was what it took to be a real man in the Mob.

Death was always close at hand and you cared nothing for anyone except number one. Life was like a ticking time bomb: one minute you could be at a party and the next minute you were being shot at or locked up in prison. You were always on the edge; there was no time to relax; you were always on guard, even when you were asleep, from internal and external rivalries. Friends and brothers died of gunshots, motorbike crashes or a bottle to the back of the head. In our minds we were living entirely for the mighty bulldog in the sky, he was our god that we would live and die for and the spectre of death was always imminent. Violence always lurked around the corner because of who we were and what we represented. But violence was our best friend and crime was the food that nourished us. We resurrected the warrior ethic of our ancestors made redundant by colonialism and reignited it generations later in a new form - without ritual, without etiquette, without rules of conduct, without tapu, without its spiritual element - distilled into an elixir of anarchic violence and brutal confrontation. We did not fight for our country, our families or any form of moral ethic; we fought purely for the patch on our back, the bulldog emblem and the colour red. When a rumble was on, the dog inside emerged to scrap - some of us could fight, others couldn't but that didn't matter because when fighting erupted the adrenaline would pump through your veins like a milking machine. Any form of warfare was admissible and it was always to the death. I became more of a dog in a rumble than at any other time - you had to or else you were in serious jeopardy. The blood of brothers that was spilt by enemies had to be revenged. Blood was life; blood was utu; blood was death. Whether we spilt our enemies blood or they spilt ours there was always silence afterwards, you never talked about it. Blood was silent, utu was silent - that was the rule after battle.

The blood of enemies, our own urine and excrement, the alcohol we drank and the sexual juices of the women we blocked stained our reggies (multiple pairs of jeans sewn together) and were signs of our mana and conquest. Our enemy's colours were sewn onto the backside of our reggies as a sign of hatred and disrespect towards them. Reggies represented the memories of all the crap in our lives and they were emblematic of our history. To wash them would be to wipe away the memory of our conquests and history.

It was a world filled with lawlessness and we were constantly paying for the consequences of our actions. But this didn't matter to us at all and least of all to me. Who cared if we went to court, got sentenced to jail or died? Prison reform, probation, anger management and all the legal paraphernalia the law created to punish those who went against the grain of society made no difference to us. Prison was our second home; it meant free kai, a pillow and a bed. And it became a haven to be schooled-up in mongrelism where we would be encouraged by the leaders and the brothers inside. Jail never reformed us back into normal society and there was nothing the establishment could do to break the spirit of the dog in us. It was inconceivable that we'd abandon the way of the dog that was our family. We would always return to our own vomit, and that vomit was a feast of violence.

Your chapter was your safe haven - the world outside could no longer save or do anything for you. We were a large family of people and many of us already had a price on our heads. We were brought up in welfare homes and borstals, reared in dysfunctional families and abused as youngsters. Some of us came from good homes too before we drifted into mongrelism. We were just plain, lonely guys without fathers or role models, floundering through a lack of encouragement or any vision for the future. Many of us were just local kids who drifted into this life because society never offered us anything different or anything to look forward to. In essence, life was boring and out of this grew the psychology of 'no future'. We were the ones who were always picked on, always copping the blame, abused, unloved, rebellious, and compromised in our childhood innocence. As the black sheep of families we in turn became the unloved, the abusers, the blame shifters, the liars, the thieves, the drunkards and the brawlers, all the by-products of a society in meltdown. We became disenfranchised non-citizens and we embraced that to the fullest.

But deep down we all wanted a place of acceptance, a place of pure comradeship and excitement - the gang seemed to be the place to meet those needs - a place where we felt accepted and at home with familiar and like-minded people. The Mob allowed us to live out a rebellion against our upbringings and the very society we hated; it was a free ticket to do anything we wanted.

To leave the gang was a serious infraction, you would be considered a traitor, a deserter, disloyal and even a coward. You became dead to the guys and it was as though you never existed.

These gang life principles set the tone for my own state of mind as a member of the Mongrel Mob for many years, every day was so unpredictable it was like living constantly on the edge. That's what made it exhilarating and exciting - it was like a fix and I craved that adrenaline rush daily. Without that fix life seemed boring.

Normal life in the gang meant continuous confrontation, the maintenance of your reputation and the administration of revenge. For instance, while sitting in the pub one day, a local just walked straight up to me and smashed me on the chin with his fist. I knew how to hold my own in those days and I failed to fall to the ground like this guy expected. I stood up and retaliated in such an aggressive manner the guy not only didn't have a chance he had no idea where the force came from. I have no idea why that local picked on me that day except maybe because I was a Mobster that represented something he didn't approve of. Maybe it was just the look in my eye he didn't like. But he picked on the wrong guy that day. Life was cheap then, you just took what was handed out and gave out what you could.

Another day, while sitting in the pub drunk on rum, I was thrown out by a security guard who thought he knew a thing or two about fighting. I threatened him that I would get him back one day. Retribution delayed. Later when I was a sandblasting labourer having worked under a bridge for a whole day, I saw the security guard riding over on a twelve-speed bike. I knew this was my chance for revenge so I caught his eye and motioned him to meet me on the riverbank. He took up my challenge and we fought with the fury of slum cats. The security guard was a martial arts expert who thought he could take me out with a few kicks. Well, he hadn't figured on the bulldog anger I harboured inside and this boosted my adrenaline levels like I'd been injected with a syringe. I knew this guy from years ago - we went to school together - but that slim bond didn't mean anything to me in my state of mind. He had wasted another brother in the Mob earlier and he had bruised my own reputation while I was drunk by throwing me out of the pub. From my point of view utu (revenge) had to be dispensed to maintain my own mana and that of the Mongrel Mob chapter I belonged to. In those days I was mentally and physically fit for any confrontation when I wasn't drunk. After a brutal battle on the riverbank I managed to overpower the guy and smash him to the point where he had to crawl home annihilated. My gang president at the time just sat and watched the fight go down. News of my victory quickly spread throughout the Mob and I began to earn a reputation as a 'true red' Mobster. I still have a permanent scar on my cheek and a bent finger as physical reminders of that fight.

The rule of law and common decency meant nothing to me then, your Mongrel Mob psyche just kicked in when an incident sparked a reaction. There were no boundaries to the behaviour of a Mobster except what the leaders said. I remember searching the streets for someone to take out my anger on after another gang acted in a manner I took as a personal affront against my own authority. I drove around this neighbourhood with one of my young followers in the passenger seat grasping a sawn-off shotgun. Identifying a gang vehicle I thought was the target we crept up beside it at the traffic lights and aimed the gun at the driver. I told the boy: 'Shoot the f .... n gun and kill the guy.' I glanced at the victim in the other car and saw the flush of fear on his face at the realisation of what was about to happen. Suddenly his vehicle sped through the smoke of screeching and burning tyres and disappeared. Full of rage I screamed at my associate for not firing on my orders. At that very moment the trigger of the gun had jammed despite multiple attempts to fire it. Frustrated and angry, I drove to the top of One Tree Hill, took the gun in my hands, pointed it to the air and pulled the trigger. The cartridges exploded and a shot was unleashed with a loud bang. The trigger was working fine now, but a chance for revenge had gone astray. In those days these sorts of incidents were normal everyday occurrences for gang members. My soul began to crave the rush of near-death experiences. I was permanently buzzing on a high and any other form of life seemed as suffocating as a poisonous mineshaft. I was true to the 'gospel of the bone' - that is to the mongrel and his ways.

Without the gangs, the media, the public and society would have no one to blame, no one to convict, no one to judge and no one to talk about. Our lives, failures and crimes were open for everyone to see - in the papers, on television, in the courts, on the streets - and there were few secrets between the Mob and the public. In some ways our lives were no different to others except we lived in big groups and our lifestyle was extreme. The antics of the Mob were visible to the public through the media and because the police were always on our case. Bad was the way we were portrayed but the public was fascinated - some would say repelled - by our image and wanted to know what we did and how we lived. We were made out to be the evil ones, which we do not hide, but we were just an abstract reflection of what the public does behind closed doors until exposed by the law and the courts.

This was my life and my 'handle' in the Mob was Bruno, a name I embraced. I soon came to realise it was a reference to the German helmet, draped with a thick chrome chain, worn by the almighty bulldog. This was the King Country chapter mascot. I thought that Bruno was quite an appropriate name. Later the women nicknamed me 'Bruising Bruno' because I loved to rumble. I adhered to the rule of the mongrel and I lived it to the hilt. The following gang motto goes to the very core of my life:

> **M**ongrels that we are
> **O**ffensive things we do
> **N**ights of bloody rumble
> **G**rowl from the old bulldog
> **R**eggies we always wear
> **E**verlasting patch
> **L**ags we do with style

Many blocks we have

Outcry from the public

Boots that we drink from!

This is not only my story but also the story of many of my brothers and sisters who have worn the patch on their back, whether for the Mongrel Mob or any other gang. It was life on the edge where death continuously lurked around every corner. Death was something I was intimate with but now it is an escape I do not flirt with and will not till it is the right time to go. I salute and remember the many brothers who have died in that state of mind trapped in a lifestyle that was sign posted No Exit. It was a life I have come to realise was void of any sense of love, respect, compassion, sympathy and decency, both for myself, my peers and anyone else. It was a lifestyle I will never forget - it was who I was then, but it is not who I am now.

True Red

'

Chapter 2
FAMILY OF ORIGIN

I was born in Wairoa on the 9th of October 1954 and named Patrick Tuhoe Isaac. My family nicknamed me Bo, the name they know me by today. I was the eighth child of a whanau of thirteen brothers and sisters. My father Jim Hohipera Isaac (Hondi) was from Tuai on Lake Waikaremoana while my mother Ngahuia Isaac (nee Hema) was from Rangiahua, a small community southwest of Wairoa. Tribally my parents were a mixture of the many hapu (sub-tribes) that make up the Ngai Tuhoe and Ngati Kahungunu tribes of those regions.

At the time I was born the whanau were living in their Tuhoe tribal region on the Tuai Valley near Lake Waikaremoana. Later the family moved into a Maori Affairs home on Ormond Road, Wairoa, opposite the railway station. This was the home I remember as the house of my childhood memories.

Dad was an ex-serviceman who served in the 28th Maori Battalion, a very strong man and a strict disciplinarian. He was also a man of the land and always had a garden full of vegetables. My earliest memory of my dad was watching him prepare the soil to plant his kumara, potatoes, kamokamo and other kai when the season came around. He believed in feeding his family well and ensuring visitors were treated with the best food and hospitality he could offer. This was the Maori way, something that was instilled into all of us as children.

My mother was always a very humble and hard working lady. She was a devoted mother and wife who always did her share of the work to keep the family ticking over. She cooked for us and made sure we were clean and that we had everything we needed as children. I remember her working in the tomato gardens in Hastings and in the shearing sheds and I always enjoyed the train rides to visit with her and share her workload. During those times Dad would take his holidays and stay at home to look after the children while mum went out to work. Like Dad, Mum was also a food gatherer and fisherwoman, she enjoyed her white-baiting when in season and gathering kaimoana (sea food). They followed after my grandparents who were proud of their vegetable garden and the different types of fruit they grew. Mum was also fond of her cards, housie and her music and she taught us the ukulele, coming as she did, from a very musical whanau. We were always well dressed, mum was always knitting and sewing for us. Brother Tom from the Catholic Church would bring the statue of Mary over to our home once or twice during the year and we would say the rosary together - after which he would give all the kids a mackintosh lollie for attending. Above everything, my parents were hard working people and there was always kai in the pot. Their strong belief to work and provide for the family always stuck in my mind and influenced my own future work ethic.

Our Maori Affairs house was built on reclaimed land that was originally a swamp. That's why it was always damp, wet and cold inside. It was no good for kids like me who were always sick, suffering from bad asthma. A spoon full of malt, castor oil, and aspro with jam were common remedies in our household for sickness. I can remember Dad always doing the washing and hanging our clothes over the fence because there was never enough room on the line. By the age of three I was touted as a cry-baby. That's why I think I had a big belly button because I cried too much and my sisters used to tease me about that. At this stage mum was feeding me with milk powder and had taken me off the breast because she was having other children. My sisters had to look after me.

Because our home was close to the railway station I remember how excited I'd be to see the big steam train pulling carriages of people into town. The station had the loveliest tasty meat pies in the world and the local fish'n'chip shop had the sweetest saveloy sausages, fish, chips and pineapple drinks. When the circus would arrive in town by train it was always a special day. The local kids would follow behind as the circus crew led the animals in to town to set up. I remember life being so simple and full of aroha (love) then.

Maori language was never spoken to us as children. I only ever heard it spoken when our parents had an argument and didn't want us kids to know what they were saying. 'Hei aha? (So What!) Hei aha?' was the phrase I heard reverberate around our house often. Looking back, it seemed like they were always arguing, probably about the heavy responsibilities of raising a big family. Mum and Dad still spoke to their whanau in te reo (Maori language) but my father was never one to speak on the marae. Mum and dad had limited education and in their day they were part of the generation punished at school if they spoke te reo Maori. Moving from the interior to Wairoa Dad made a decision not to speak Maori; he wanted to encourage his family to live in the Pakeha world from that time on. He believed the only way the next generation would survive was to learn the ways of the Pakeha. The prevailing wisdom in those days was to walk in the ways of the Pakeha and for our generation that meant an emphasis on English language and education and a drift away from our own native tongue and culture. This is something many of us lament now, not being able to understand our own language and the ways of our people. With the wisdom of hindsight it alienated us from our traditions.

Living near the Wairoa River was certainly picturesque but it was a place not only of life but also of death, depending on the way you respected the river. The river was steeped in an ancestral history you could sometimes feel hovering in the air. In the summertime the tourists used to watch us kids slide down the grey muddy banks of the Wairoa River to the water. Often the kids from our street would swim across the river to the Ruataniwha district to take fruit from the trees in a paddock there. One day my sisters swam across the river to pick fruit and left me on the riverbank by myself. Not wanting to miss out on the fun I followed them and eventually jumped into the river. I was swiftly dragged downstream and I remember being swept into a whirlpool. Bubbles swirled around my head, I was sinking and I began swallowing mouthfuls of water. All I remember was my left hand going up into the air to reach for help as everything turned to darkness. Miraculously a neighbour happened to be standing on the bank and he saw me, grabbed my hand and pulled me out of the river. Within seconds I was out of the water safely on the bank. I'll never forget that spot - it was my mother's favourite white-baiting location. My life had stood in the balance, a balance between light and dark. I remember now how Mum had always warned me to be careful of that spot.

Our home was always filled with people, both those we knew well and others we really had little knowledge about. We always had relations staying and others who befriended my father came and went. A guy who was an acquaintance of the whanau would often visit our home leaving his bags behind while he went to work. Sometimes he would take me for a ride in his car to a secluded place. Here we would play 'special games' together. I remember having to perform sexual acts on him. These were his 'special games', games that were even initiated in our own home. I never shared any of this with my parents and to this day my family still do not know.

If I was to consider what effect this had on my life I would say it awakened something in me that should never have arisen at that age. I became very sexually aware and active from that time on. All sorts of sexual encounters seemed to follow me around. It was like a newly formed lustful mind would search for any opportunity for a sexual encounter. It may have also been the beginning of my distrust of adults and the planting of the seed of hate towards society.

Having just started at North Clyde school, I remember a nine-year-old local Wairoa girl leading me to a paddock at the back of our house where she lay a coal sack on the ground and coaxed me into playing sex games. Over the next seven years I became sexually promiscuous with my school friends, and neighbours, and many of the kids from our region participated in heavy petting and sex games together. Because these encounters were so frequent they were normalised in the minds of the kids in the neighbourhood.

As a youngster I was always very sports oriented. At the age of seven I joined the local Kahungunu gym where I learnt to box. My father rigged up a bag with sand in it at home that we used as a punching bag. He tied it to the big branch of the peach tree. Dad taught me to box and it was a common sport in the schools then. I excelled at it and later I was able to utilize this talent in my adult gang life. Later I joined the Wairoa boxing gym, where my love of the sport grew. I would often run ten kilometres a day. I plunged myself into other local sports like rowing, gymnastics, rugby and athletics. My talent in the ring and my savage right hook allowed me to travel to places like Gisborne, Patea, New Plymouth and Waipukurau to team boxing tournaments. These sports trips somehow sanctioned the assistant coach to select boys in the team to sit in the front of the van with him and this turned out to be a ploy he used to get close to us. Usually these were overnight trips where we were billeted out. I was always paired with this guy and billeted in homes where we were given a single room with two beds to sleep in. During the evenings he would sexually molest me almost without fail. At first I had no control over what was happening, but I never fought his urges and slowly I began to like the attention he showed me over time. He slowly and subtly gained my confidence as we drove together, trained together, and fought together. I was considered an above average sportsman and was eventually selected as an exhibition fighter against an Australian opponent in Hawkes Bay. I was ecstatic when I won on points. This assistant coach would organise ways and means to accompany me to away fights so he could spend time with me. The fight, the sweat, the young athletic bodies, the bare skin and the smell of liniment must have ignited the coach's hormones; it became quickly apparent that this was the perfect place to feed his warped sexual urges. This relationship carried on for about a year but I never told anyone in the family what was happening in my life, I kept it to myself. My attitude was Hei aha? So What? Who cares!

During my school years I became a sexual predator myself with the local neighbourhood girls, taking them to secret places where we could experiment with each other. There were also experimental brushes with male friends my own age. Revealingly, now I look back on it, most of my circle of friends from Wairoa who had similar sexual backgrounds also became Mobsters. My confidence and youthful sexual activity soon gave me the idea I was God's gift to women; love was never part of the equation.

I'm not sure why I never said a word to anyone about what had happened to me, maybe it was because I thought this was simply normal family behaviour and everyone acted like this. The one thing I do remember is how the adults around me never taught us anything about sexuality. Maybe the subject was regarded as tapu or maybe it was just something not spoken about in New Zealand families in those days. None of the adults around us ever informed us of what was acceptable or unacceptable in terms of sexuality, it was something joked about but never taught. The result was I had little knowledge about what was sexually right or wrong and the parameters of my own sexuality were left entirely up to me to define. Looking back, I've always wondered whether the eyes of the older generation were either shut to what was happening or distracted in the battle to keep their heads above water. This is not a criticism of my parent's standard of upbringing because I know they loved me and did their best for me with what they had. However, I believe the society we were raised in was neglectful. From all the discussions I've had with people who lived a similar life to me, it seems my parent's generation were living with blinkers on, and either willfully or absent-mindedly, didn't know what was going on. The number of people I have met of my generation or older who were sexually abused without anyone taking any protective steps or recognising what was happening still astounds me. Our fathers, if they were around, were the hunter-providers for the family, and our mothers were the ones to teach us life skills. But sexual knowledge and relationships were never ever taught to my generation; we had to find our own pathway, a pathway in many cases that became detrimental to our lives.

My early sexual encounters, whether it was at the hands of someone else or personally initiated, laid down a template that was to be mirrored in the way I treated men and women for the rest of my life. Further down the road, I would be accused of sexual violation and rape, accusations that seemed to follow me all the days of my life.

Chapter Three
DOING THE LAG

I left home at the age of fifteen to start my education as a sheet metal worker in Auckland. This was organised under the Maori Trade Training Scheme where many young Maori from rural regions left their homes, lived in the city and learnt a trade. My father sent me on my new life journey with $20 in my hand and a bag of clothes over my shoulder. There were eight of us from Wairoa College in 1969 that left home and caught the New Zealand Railways bus to begin new careers in the city. Arriving in Auckland I had never seen so many buildings, lights, cars and people. I was excited about the new adventures ahead and felt safe having my mates around me. We stayed at Tumanako Hostel on Domett Avenue in Epsom and attended Auckland Technical Institute (A.T.I.) for our daytime trade studies. The hostel was to be home for those doing the three Maori and Polynesian trade apprenticeships - carpentry, sheet metal and plumbing - and it was here that I began a five-year apprenticeship.

During the day we studied and in the evenings we frequented the pubs. Often we visited the museum on the weekends. Some of the boys knew how to strum a guitar and it became a catalyst for many a party. On Sundays it was compulsory for all hostel boarders to attend an Anglican church service - a bus was supplied as transport - even though on most mornings we were suffering from hangovers you could photograph. Church was boring, it didn't really mean anything to us and was just part of the deal. Lunch on Sunday was usually roast mutton with puddings of jelly and ice cream. I loved those meals.

Misbehaviour meant being 'gated' or restricted from leaving the premises except for training work. Along with the partying, drinking and arriving home late I also had a problem with stealing, a habit I picked up from my Wairoa school peers and neighbourhood friends. I remember being 'gated' for three weeks, which seemed at the time like a small eternity. It was often a lonely life coming, as we did, from small Maori rural communities, separated from families and living in a place foreign to us. We all suffered from homesickness. After six months of bad homesickness I contemplated leaving and I was very depressed for much of that time. In fact, most of us suffered from depression for periods of time. That aside, a very close brotherly comradeship grew out of our separation from whanau. This was some consolation and we all became inseparable.

But, there were precious moments that took my mind off home. Travelling on the bus from the hostel to tech one day I met up with a young Maori girl from Auckland Girls Grammar. I found out her name was Cookie, she was beautiful and had a fair complexion for a Maori. Even though we only had a brief conversation that was enough to send me head-over-heels in love. She was the only thing on my mind for days. I wandered around the hostel and tech in a daze, her image firmly imprinted on my brain like a re-touched studio photograph. Even the boys thought I was acting strangely. It was the first time I experienced what having a crush on someone was like. Every morning I caught the bus I became obsessed with catching a glimpse of Cookie and sometimes she was there, other times she wasn't. When she was on the bus I would admire her from a distance. Nothing came of it, but its significance was profound: I became aware I had true love feelings for the opposite sex and I'd never experienced this before. Other encounters with female friends had never given me that almost suffocating throbbing in my throat that I had with Cookie.

After my first year of sheet metal training at ATI I chose to go to Palmerston North to complete my apprenticeship. The decision to move to the Manawatu was not work-based but more about following a girl. At this point in my life I remember beginning to move further away from my family and I began to seek whanaungatanga (relationship), friendship and companionship in strange places. In my naivety I thought the love, proximity and support I no longer had with my family I could find in relationships with the opposite sex.

In 1971 I spent nine months in Palmerston North with Berry's Engineers as an apprentice. I left this place as I had lost interest in my work. I then found a job with Richardson Drilling, a private drilling rig company. As an apprentice I was given every dirty low-life job you could think of and I couldn't be bothered with it in the end. After reading an Australian Post magazine advertising the Gold Coast, with pictures of sand, surf and scantily clad women, I decided to get out of this place and leave for Australia. But a sixteen-year-old Maori teenager arriving alone in Sydney with nothing was a brave move. I caught a taxi and asked the driver to take me to a place where I would find Maori people. I washed up in Kings Cross and leaving my bags at St Vincent de Paul's I searched the streets to find accommodation. At the Hampton Court Hotel I met some Maori guys who put me up till I could find my feet and a job in this strange new land. Eventually, I scored a sheet metal job in Zetland for three months, but after an altercation with the bosses I found myself working on the circus and carnival circuit. At that point I changed my name to Tara Rangi. The name was based on another Maori guy who worked this circuit, a strong man with a huge appetite. I liked the character of this man and I not only took on his name but his persona - eating a lot and acting tough - even though I was a slightly built teenager. Using an alias was common among the carnival workers as most of them were ex-prisoners or criminals. The carnival environment was hard physical work with many transients and our carnival circuit was strung out around the Sydney suburbs. For most of my circus work life I was stationed at the go-karts or at the Ferris wheel. The go-karts were always very popular, but it was heavy work building the track, maintaining the movement of cars, and controlling the enormous flow of people. Often we had to deal with public nuisances, particularly the skinheads, and sometimes provocation erupted into a brawl. But working with a wide range of people, meeting different cultures and travelling was a great lifestyle and I enjoyed it. Living on site with the carnival meant adhering to a code of work ethics: getting into trouble was out, public safety was crucial, the mechanical maintenance of the rides was paramount and any abuse of people or property meant you were out on your ear. Socially, carnival life was like one big happy family; we drank together, worked together, and watched out for each other's backs. It was like - now I think back on it - living in a gang.

Travelling to different suburbs meant setting up camp, checking out the local pubs, mixing with the locals and eyeing up the women. Alcohol played a large part in the social life and it prevailed everywhere we went. Young girls not under parental guidance, who had run away from home or were living on the streets, were always attracted to the carnival environment and they frequented the after hours parties we ran. The pretty girls who partied with us always got free rides: 'A free ride for a free ride,' as we used to say. The girls who became our favourites became our possessions.

One incident over a young woman I became possessive about sent me over the edge. When I returned to her home one night I was confronted by her father who took one look at me and ordered me off the premises, abusively telling me to leave his daughter alone. Provoked, I reacted violently with no thought of the consequences. The police were called immediately and I found myself amidst a blaze of flashing lights and police dogs, and later a putrid police cell. I was sentenced to a lag in Parramatta prison with three months hard labour. What contributed to my imprisonment was the strong anti-Maori feeling in Australia at the time: we were just 'no hopers' and 'bludgers' and this made my court appearance an uneasy experience.

Parramatta prison was a harrowing experience. I was transported with six or seven other prisoners in a hot, stinking police van and presented to the receiving officer who decked us out with uniforms, dixie-plates for dinner and pudding, and a bucket for our human waste. As part of the de-humanising process we were each given a number to replace our names. My number is to this day tattooed on my brain: P1490. The saunter to my cell was a hard thing to take, but I wasn't going to let any emotions, particularly fear, even register on my face. The place was putrid and reeked of a heady mix of human waste and disinfectant that opened up your nasal passages to a smell that to this day still lingers. As I walked into my cellblock loneliness hit me like a sideshow sledgehammer as a hundred eyes stabbed me in the back; I wondered why I ever left home. I was seventeen and life in this prison was hard. I just had to take it as it came and I am not ashamed to say I counted every day off till I was freed. Because I was alone I had to watch my back, learn to roll with the punches and take things as they came. There were a number of challenges I had to deal with in prison, mostly from other inmates, guys who were in there for life. The lifers were dangerous as they didn't care what they did - they were there for life so they tried to set you up and have fun at your expense. One old man arranged for me to bunk-in with him. He was very hospitable, serving tea and sandwiches and befriending me with mollifying words. However, while I was asleep one night I could feel hands creeping over my body. The old man was trying to have his way with me, so I grabbed his wrist and twisted his arm up his back and told him never to touch me again. He wasn't strong but the old man had a well-honed streak of ruthlessness that persuaded him to take revenge on me for not accepting his advances. Unexpectedly, I heard my number called out over the loudspeaker summoning me to the infirmary. Unusual, I thought. But I obeyed the bosses' call and made my way through the corridors to the infirmary. But, it was a set up by the lifers and the old man was hiding behind a wall with an iron bar ready to crack my head open. As I walked along I just happened to see him out of the corner of my eye, so when he swung at me I was able to restrain him and turn the tables. I was able to overpower him and send him packing. My boxing certainly came in handy in prison. From that point on he never tried anything on me again and the only thing that came my way from the infirmary after that was ointment to heal the scabies I caught from the blankets in my cell.

You had to toughen up quickly inside or else you'd end up becoming a rag doll for some low life. Being in a confined space with hardened criminals - lifers, rapists, drug dealers and robbers - would influence my whole life. I remember the way these guys controlled the prison and it scared me. Life was harsh and I found it expedient to just shut my mouth and stay out of trouble. I would hear the schemes the guys wanted to action when they got out, crimes to be committed not only in Australia but also in New Zealand. I found one Maori guy in the prison who I related to and I was glad in my heart I'd found someone I could connect with. Intriguingly, I was to meet up with him again later in a New Zealand prison. In the end I had to get close to the Aussie blokes inside; they were cheeky and held strongly to their convict histories as a way of giving meaning to their lives.

After three weeks I was handcuffed along with eight other guys in a prison van and sent on a stifling 15-hour drive to Glen Innes Minimum Security Prison Camp to do hard labour. I was pleased to be in an open-air situation where freedom could at least be dreamed of, rather than being confined to a claustrophobic prison where only grey, dull colours predominated, giving you a sense you'd never leave the place. The camp I arrived at was made up of small bach type sheds where the prisoners lived. The days were filled with hard labour in searing heat, clearing bush, and breaking up rocks for pavements and roads in some never-to-be sighted suburbia. The flip-side was you lost weight and got fit fast. The driving focus for this camp was to teach you the morals and ethics of society through hard labour and I was placed in a team ruled by a hard-assed prison screw. It was a mentally, physically and emotionally overwhelming no-life situation for me as a teenager and I did my best to try and come to terms with it.

Along with the hardships of the hard manual labour you were also constantly dealing with dysfunctional inmates: guys with short wicks, anger problems and barely suppressed tempers. I had to look at them, associate with them, talk to them, work with them and do recreation with them and this was always potentially inflammatory especially when brawls occurred and the screws turned a blind eye. This allowed the guys to sort out the weak from the strong and create a vicious hierarchical system among the inmates.

I tried to create a relationship with the aborigines inside but they were volatile - they could gang up on you and give you the bash with little warning. They were hard to trust because you never knew how to take those brothers. But I proved myself to them on the sports field where I played hard and fast for their side.

The guys doing short lags took it hard as their minds were always on their family, wondering how they were coping on the outside. It was a harsh learning process but I was determined to do my lag silently and get on with the job.

In time I was released from prison knowing nobody and with nowhere to go. Five of us were freed at the same time and we celebrated our release day in the pub at Glenn Innes. Reaching Parramatta by train we decided to continue our celebration with a real bout of binge drinking. A couple of Maori guys at one particular pub took pity on me and invited me to stay with them. They found me employment with them making fridges. We worked hard by day and drank hard by night. Living this kind of lifestyle, I found myself at parties with all sorts of people including members of the local bikie gang. One night these guys arrived at our pad to party, bringing one of their women with them who was eventually blocked (gang raped) during the course of the evening. At the time I was off my face asleep in a car parked outside. However, I was one of five guys arrested for rape, taken to the police cells and placed on remand back at Parramatta Prison. Despite my protests of innocence no one was listening to this Maori boy. When we eventually arrived at the courthouse the witness did not appear and fortuitously the charges were dropped. Sure, the charges did not stick but accusations of rape were to follow me in the future like a persistent apparition. This apparition transmogrified into a permanent monkey on my back and caused me havoc everywhere I was to go.

In Australia I seemed to lose something within myself, maybe it was a loss of innocence or the theft of my true identity. I wasn't Patrick anymore, I wasn't Bo anymore or Tara Rangi, I was simply a number. But one thing was for sure, I was moving in a direction that was sending me further and further away from my whanau. Additionally, the Australian experience became prophetic of a future life pathway that seemed almost set in stone - being a hardened and lawless criminal locked down behind bars was going to be my lot. The seeds of my conditioning were beginning to sprout. Beyond this, deep-seated homesickness and loneliness was eating my soul and a void opened up like a tooth cavity that craved to be filled. This persuaded me to return home.

In 1973 I left Sydney and flew to Wellington to stay with my eldest brother and his partner. I found staying with him very hard and it felt like I had lost all connection with my whanau and friends. Maybe I had changed so much I was no longer one of the whanau except by name, whakapapa (genealogy) and DNA. In reality, I did not want to return to the arms of my family and burden them with my shame; I didn't want them to paper over the cracks; I wanted to find my own way of dealing with my life and assuming my own responsibilities. Maybe if I had humbled myself and returned home I could have diverted the anguish I'd caused them and myself. This was not to be.

Instead I started drinking at the local pubs in Wellington where I met up with a number of old schoolmates who were either in the Mongrel Mob or Black Power. Their comradeship and the way the boys duplicated a whanau of like-minded brothers really appealed to me. My spirit seemed to empathise with the gang situation and lifestyle. Following in the footsteps of my schoolmates I joined the Mongrel Mob and began to 'prospect' for the Wellington chapter.

Chapter Four
BOTTOM ROCKER

The way we heard it - the Mongrel Mob gang originated in the Hawkes Bay, spread to Wairoa, then moved to Wellington and on to the Manawatu. It was originally a whanau-based group. However, when this gang of guys numbered over a thousand we were increasingly thought of as terrorists. In March 1973, I became affiliated with the Wellington chapter of the Mongrel Mob that meant rearranging my mindset on many things. I'd been used to acting alone and individualistically but now there was the safety umbrella of numbers. Entering the gang meant submerging who I really was and picking up a whole new set of ideals. But I was a prime candidate for the gang lifestyle: I now had a persona that shouted dangerous, lost, lonely, and up for a fight against established society and the world.

At that time Gummy was the president of the Wellington chapter, a tall, lanky Samoan brother. Their pad was dark; the red flag flew with the emblem of the dog in all its glory. Beer crates festooned the premises filled with Lion Red and Lion Brown beer, and the guitar would be singing all day long. The guys in this Mob were huge and tough, scruffy and mean, wearing steel-capped working boots from their jobs as truckies and demolition workers. The three stars tattooed on the side of the face signified that the guys were from a borstal background. Our heavy boots, the long trench coats and the Stetson hats decorated with red scarves were our defining fashion in those days.

I had to prove myself as a prospect worthy to enter into the chapter by literally fighting my way into the hearts of the gang members, stealing cars and committing other petty crimes. Having a prior prison record and an association with many of the boys allowed me to be more easily accepted as part of the gang. Alcohol was what sealed our brotherhood and we drank in the pubs and the pad, even with the Black Power guys. It was the beginning of my road to perdition.

I received my patch with the bulldog image in the centre, the Mongrel Mob logo on the top rim and the district spelt out on the 'bottom rocker' or lower rim of the patch. The Wellington Mob emblem was a bulldog with no helmet, an image I also had tattooed on my left lower arm. We were stationed at Newtown but there were other chapters in the greater Wellington area - Upper Hutt, Lower Hutt, Petone and Porirua. The continual drinking and partying cemented me as one of the team.

What became 'trendy' in gang lifestyle was 'blocking', where women would be gang raped by the boys. It almost became the trademark of the Mongrel Mob then - something I had only previously witnessed in Australia - and my immersion began when I entered the Wellington chapter. It was usually initiated in the pubs but continued later at the gang pads. When the opportunity presented itself to be part of a 'block' with the Wellington Mob I was unashamedly desperate to get my rocks off. For me, having been in Australia, jailed twice, and filled with a deep-seated anger against the world it was payday. And I was going to take it out on the woman the gang had lined up. After waiting hours for my turn I entered the room to find a young woman - unwashed, covered in semen, blood and sexual juices, and reeking of sexual aroma and alcohol - waiting for the next taker. The sex was forceful and impersonal, anything went and there was only one rule: no names were ever to be spoken. Guys would slap your backside to urge you on as they stood around watching the spectacle. If the woman didn't perform for whatever reason - inebriation or being wasted on drugs - it was nothing a punch in the head or a black eye wouldn't fix. It was considered cool to be involved in a block but weak for it to become loving or intimate. This form of sex - whether you want to call it a 'block' or a rape - was the norm to us.

My first block was aggressive and strangely satisfying, enabling me to get my rocks off after an arid period in a sexual desert. I walked out of this encounter with my reggies stained with bodily fluids, never to be washed again. The stained fabric spoke of my conquest and reputation and it was a form of initiation into the code of the gang. The more unwashed, the more you were considered one of the Mob. Blocking was never considered to be rape because it was viewed as consensual irrespective of the fact that violence invariably rode in tandem with the act. Occasionally women taken to the block protested, but they were simply overpowered and told: 'If you want to hang out with the Mob, then you're fair game.' That, in a nutshell, was the hard and fast rule of the gang and everyone, including the young women that hung out with the guys, knew what could occur and what was expected.

Other times the women instigated the block in the hope of having sex with the top man which was something to gossip about with others later. The higher the rank of the Mobster, the more sexually attractive you were to all sorts of women - young, old, white and brown.

According to our Mob mentality men were superior to women in every way and women had to respect that. To my mind, if they were willing to hang out in this environment they had embraced our ethic and that included the institution of the block. Women were fair game, we owned them, and they were delegated on a whim to cook our eggs, look after our children or satisfy our sexual desires.

Just as the guys had to go through the heavy and violent process of prospecting to accumulate recognition and eventually earn their patch, the women had to endure the block both as a form of duty and initiation. Without exception everyone knew what was expected; this was naked survival and it gave you status and favour amongst the members. In essence, it was seen as a form of knowing you were wanted, needed and even loved by the guys. And in a curious irony, some girls who were blocked felt good about their badness. Most occasions were private and they were always unsafe: no contraceptives, no washing, no protection and no boundaries. Heterosexual sex was the norm but on that broad canvas was painted group sex, penetration in any and every orifice, violence, aggression, sadism, and occasionally, skirting heterosexual sex, bestiality.

Girls, women or just hangers-on who turned up to our pad, parties and other functions were labelled 'wenches' or 'scrubbers' and not only were they fair game but they belonged, like a communal harem, to everyone. To this day I remain amazed at the number of beautiful young teenage girls who entered our premises of their own free will and practically opened their legs for all the brothers. I myself took advantage of this situation many times - why wouldn't I? What is offered should be duly received.

My own observation is that these young women were attracted to what the gang life offered, something that was absent in their own homes or in society. Some craved for fathers and brothers, or simply to be associated with an adventurous, exciting, tough and rebellious group that put a bit of zip into a mundane, boring or violent home life. We were open to their needs but strictly under Mob rules. The inner warrior spirit, or what we perceived it to be, attracted hundreds of young women into our circle. We never ever had to search for women; they flocked to us in droves. As far as we were concerned the women wanted what we offered them as a gang and as men. In our gang society we had hundreds of girls, some as young as fourteen, who would openly lie on the block for us every day, even when we weren't in the mood.

Respect for these women was only occasioned when one of the boys 'claimed' a blocked woman as his own and the president sanctioned it. From that time on a claimed woman was no longer up for the block. That is not to say she wouldn't be blocked if her man allowed the guys to share his partner. In fact, this was common practice. According to the Mob precepts, women were simply for pleasure. When guys were sent to do their lag in prison, their wives, girlfriends, daughters and mothers were fair game to be 'serviced' by the brothers on the outside. Even gang leaders who were sent to prison could not control this; they could not protect their families from the inside. Brutal as it sounds, that was just the Mob rule.

My predatory sexual instincts could be lived out in the gang and I became addictively covetous of women. I was now in an environment where sex and women were available at any time, provided you waited your turn. Like beer, sex was on tap and there was never any shortage of girls or women who wanted to hang-out and be blocked.

My life in Wellington became erratic and I couldn't seem to stay in one place for more than a month or two; I had a permanent case of itchy feet and I developed a particulary restless disposition. I remember travelling to Palmerston North to hopefully reconnect with old friends only to find many of them were already in the Manawatu Mob chapter. The upshot was that I allied myself with these guys for a season.

The Manawatu president at the time was a very staunch and mean leader. I was made a Manawatu patched member by attending their functions, and parties. This was a chapter in warfare mode with another local bikie gang. The majority of the bikie guys were Pakeha. Fighting was common and we always had to watch our backs walking in the streets, driving around town or even going to the movies.

I was here for nearly a year from 1974 to 1975. In a fairly short space of time I had become more and more immersed in pure 'mongrel' thinking; the Mob was beginning to mean everything to me on the outside, while on the inside I remained lonely. Unable to stay too long in one place I was always searching for something to quench my soul's yearning for true intimacy, companionship and love. Sometimes I think I was so desensitised to the feelings of true whanau, spiritual love and intimacy, that to come back to zero seemed impossible.

Getting itchy feet again I moved up to Auckland with a Pakeha friend whose 'handle' was The Gypsy, a really solid and loyal brother to me. On the trip up we partied up a storm all the way. At Auckland I was locked up for stealing money from a cabin on one of the boats we ended up partying on. I saw the police board the boat so I slid down the rope that moored the ship and accidentally fell into the sea. Drunk, I thought I was going to drown, but miraculously I somehow managed to pull myself to safety on the wharf. I was caught at the gates of the wharf and locked in the police cells where I slept heavily until I was brought to stand before the judge the next day. He stood me down on remand for a report and to be sentenced. In the end I pleaded guilty to the charges and was sentenced to three months imprisonment for burglary.

I was transferred from Mt Eden Prison to Rangipo Prison Camp just outside of Turangi at the beginning of the Desert Road. Once again this lag was hard labour, cutting firewood in the bush and farming. It was a minimum-security prison in an outdoor location - very cold in winter and extremely hot in summer. But, there were a lot more outdoor activities here than in other prisons. Being imprisoned with Kiwi inmates was very different to my Australian experience. While the Aussies were cheeky and smart, the brothers in New Zealand came from a more whanau-based mindset where you were brothers forever through your prison experience.

Most of the inmates here graduated through the New Zealand borstal system of bad boys. The lock-down was easier - from 9pm to 7am. The good thing about Rangipo for me was the level of networking I was able to achieve with new brothers and old gangsters and these 'hook ups' proved fruitful in the future.

After my three months in Rangipo Prison, I was released and eventually made my way to Taumarunui in the King Country in December 1975. I found a place with the new chapter there under the leadership of newly selected president, Porky. Digger was the vice-president and Jinx the sergeant-of-arms.

The gang pad was situated on an old family property, near Kaitupeka Marae, we called 'The Battlefield.' It was here I committed wholeheartedly to the chapter. This meant presenting myself at a meeting to say who I was and to quote my past. While I was accepted I still had to fight hand-to-hand combat with some of the guys, and survive it, to acquire my patch. It was common for guys in my position to fight six guys all at once and if you were still standing after one minute hard rumbling you had earned the right to wear the patch. Stepped out to fight one-on-one was common at The Battlefield but there were never any hard feelings between guys in a rumble, it was just part of the culture. I remember the president showing his bravery by having the guys shoot at a German helmet with a .22 rifle while he was still wearing it. On another occasion I saw him smash a full flagon of beer over his own head and come out of it uninjured. I saw him stab his own hand and not even wince. I always admired Porky then, I still do to this day.

We canvassed the idea of assuming the Mongrel Mob title for our gang with members of Porky's whanau and Maori elders (kaumatua) from the region. The local elders were very disparaging about taking on the name and some thought it the 'work of the devil'. They thought that if we assumed this name it could be a curse.

Nevertheless, the King Country Mongrel Mob chapter was formed and we made the name our own. One thing I remember about the face of our gang was how young we were venturing into a world that would be both dangerous and exciting. To become fully recognised we had to receive or earn the blessing of the more established gang chapters in the Wellington district and as part of the team I travelled down to Porirua and on to Wellington to seek sanction for our existence. Just as I had to fight to receive my patch, the gang had to win a ritual fight to prove our own separate mana. To advance our staunchness Porky and the team entered the White Heron Pub and tried to step out the entire place, but no one there accepted the challenge, which gave us a victory by default. However, at Porirua our vice-president Digger rumbled with one member of the local chapter and laid him to waste. The fact that the Porirua president stopped any retaliation and said 'let it go' gave credence and momentum to the Taumarunui chapter's continuation. As a side-bar to the trip, on the return home we picked up a woman who happened to be hitchhiking to Wanganui and blocked her. The whole event was the chapter's baptism of life. We celebrated our existence at a 1976 New Year celebration at the Ngakaunui Community Hall with Porky's whanau.

Porky was an interesting character, well versed in the reo and local tikanga and very family orientated. At whanau-based events he would encourage us to dance and mix freely with his whanau.

Days later in early January 1976 an eighteen-year-old Pakeha girl was blocked by Mongrel Mob members in Taumarunui, King Country. She was an associate of another local gang we had made a truce with to stop fighting each other. We turned up to one of their parties and during the evening the young woman was shunted on to the block. She was already associated with one of our guys but did not consent to the rest of the brothers' debauchery. On January 4th 1976, during the police enquiry, a major confrontation took place between the police and our Mob chapter. While we gathered down by the riverside a few miles out of town, partying up large, the police arrived to ask questions. A firearm was produced and fired at the police on their arrival and they were aggressively told to leave.

The police left the scene only to call for back-up from the armed offenders squad. The Mongrel Mob tried to return to Taumarunui township to regroup and gather forces, only to be confronted by a roadblock set up on the Taringa-motu straight.

Porky showed his trademark phlegmatic staunchness and set-off on a courageous and arrogant saunter straight through the police roadblock. Guns pointing at him, he led the gang through the blockade and into Taumarunui unharmed. As a leader he showed his true colours at that moment and secured the younger Mobster's unrelenting respect and mine.

During the day a number of police arrests were made and four members were shunted into the police cells. I was one of the 'dogs' arrested. Eventually, the gang made a pact to break us all out of the police cells. Around about 2.30pm that day the Mob gathered in front of the police station. Shots were fired by the Mob to scare the police. But in the return fire from the armed offenders squad our gang sergeant-of-arms Jinx, still only a teenager, was shot and fatally wounded. From the cells we heard the shots but did not know the full ramifications until later when news reached us that Jinx had died. Inside we contemplated utu and discussed ways to kill the police; as far as we were concerned they were the scum of the earth, just pigs that we had no time or respect for.

This sparked off a Mob verses police rumble which ended with the police overpowering the gang and a further twenty Mongrel Mob members were arrested. The whole twenty-four of us were on various charges ranging from unlawful assembly, attempted murder to rape. The majority of us were in our early twenties and a few were still in their late teens. This was a crucial engagement for us and it sealed the creation and identity of the Taumarunui chapter of the Mongrel Mob, nowadays known as the Mongrel Mob King Country.

The event was yet another version of initiation into the Mongrel Mob and it is difficult to think of another single incident that did as much to cement my total adherence to gang life as this. Sure, Jinx's death was sad and hard to take but at the same time it was exhilarating and very public. While on remand at Wanganui Prison we lamented the calamitous death of Jinx and it galvanised us into composing a poem in commemoration of his life:

'Trust no cunt, man, woman, or beast,

Mongrel Mob memories no one can steal,

Your death left a wound that no one could heal,

Some may forget now that you are gone,

But the Mob will remember, no matter how long.'

His death affected all of us inside and personally I wear a tattoo on my left forearm in memory of him to this day. It is a Mongrel emblem with the words RIP JINX on a scroll, a sword and a cross. This scroll remembers his name and the date of his death as one of the true martyrs of the Mob. The sword symbolises his position as sergeant-of-arms while the cross speaks of the memory of his death. While we sat on remand waiting for our court hearings, I was privileged to have my back tattooed with the Taumarunui chapter bulldog emblem at the hands of all the guys including Porky, Pup, and Skunk. It was all done by hand with crude 'boob' fashioned instruments - sewing needles inserted into matchsticks bound with black cotton thread which absorbed the ink. When the needle pierced the skin it drew blood and the ink was impregnated into the skin. Two guys worked on me at any one time and it was finally completed over a month or so. It was my permanent patch - a bulldog wearing 'Da Bruno' - a German helmet. This proved my allegiance to the King Country Mob forever. That was who I was. What made it special was having the brothers each create a section of this permanent patch with ink and I viewed this act as a total acceptance on behalf of the brothers. Since then my body has been tattooed many times with different emblems of the bulldog as a witness of gang allegiance and as indelible milestones of what was happening in my life at the time.

We never attended Jinx's funeral - we were locked-down - but there were many discussions about our actions and our loyalty to the Mongrel Mob.[i] At the tangi some of the parents of the guys said they had tried to impress on their children the wrongs of their ways but these warnings had not been heeded. Other elders wanted us to discard the name and the attitude of the Mob. Apparently the minister conducting the funeral service asked the Maori communities to examine the causes and attitudes that led to Jinx's death. He believed that the community needed to provide the young with love and security lest they seek it somewhere else like in gang membership.[2]

Twenty of us were charged with a number of crimes ranging from rape, indecent assault, unlawful assembly and attempted murder to stealing the victim's licence. Most of us were released on bail. However, Porky, Skunk and Pup were kept on remand in the Wanganui Prison. I lied and gave the cops an alias as I knew they would not be able to trace me to any previous criminal record. Bail was easily arranged.

I found myself staying with Porky's parents for a small period of time. Their home was just above The Battlefield and was an earthen floor whare (house) with an old wooden wet-back fire stove. I remember the kiore (rats) running through the roof and the rakiraki (ducks) always searching for food outside. Porky's dad took me hunting goats and returning from the bush we had to hang the meat up to pawhara (cut and dry) it. I considered the old man a righteous man who lived a simple Maori lifestyle, hunting from the forest for food to feed his family. And, the family truly did live off the land. He spoke freely to me one day about a story from the Paipera Tapu (Bible). From the book of Genesis he spoke of how Joseph was set up by his master for spurning Potiphar's wife's sexual advances. She lied to her husband that Joseph had acted inappropriately with her and he was thrown into jail. In jail for many years God nevertheless had a specific plan for Joseph's life. Eventually Joseph became one of the rulers of Egypt and was reunited with his family. This story always stuck in the back of my mind, even though I never really fully comprehended the full impact of that story except that some guy called Joseph, who lived thousands of years ago, went to jail for a sexual crime he never committed. I'm not sure why the old man shared that story with me - he may have been more intuitive than I realised at the time. Neither did I know it at the time that Joseph's saga would duplicate itself uncannily in my life over the years to come.

The result of the Wanganui Supreme Court rape hearing saw three of us sentenced to five years incarceration. Because Porky was the 'head man' he received six years in a maximum security prison. I would serve three years and nine months of this sentence, a lag that would harden my heart at the same time as it prepared me for a greater role in the gang.

True Red

Chapter Five
INSIDE PAREMOREMO

I was sent to Mount Eden Prison before being classified and moved to Paremoremo Maximum Security Prison. There were rumors in Mt Eden about how hard and tough it was to serve time at Paremoremo. It was a different breed of prisoner at this maximum security prison or so I heard. But that didn't mean a thing to me; I was a Mobster and I believed that we were not only the toughest but bullet-proof. Additionally, I was in the safe company of my brothers and they were my source of strength. Entering Paremoremo after the drive from Auckland we were stripped, showered, given our kit locker and 'boob' gear, sent to classification, given a number and had the rules laid down to us by the screws. Essentially, they said we could either obey the rules and do it easy or do it hard; it was our decision how we did our time. Maximum security was for the worst criminals who have committed violent crimes such as rape, murder and robbery. It was the place for 'lifers' and an assortment of the most dangerous guys in the country; it didn't get any tougher than this. Double-grilled doors were everywhere, right from the entrance to the prison to the 'porch' that we called the dog cage. Cameras were everywhere.

The prison screws were hard men in themselves, tough guys, mostly ex-army or ex-SAS. They were also very mentally alert; they had to be considering the calibre of guys they had to control. I remember at first having to earn the respect of the screws, but later this one-way street was reversed as more and more Mobsters began to enter the prison system. To control this burgeoning gang roll call and ensure the prison's easy running the screws had to forge good relationships with us.

I spent my twenty first birthday in prison, but that didn't mean anything to anyone except me; it was considered weak to celebrate a birthday in prison or any other place for that matter. So I just noted it in my mind and had my own private party with no one else to celebrate it with. To survive here I had to become more of a Mongrel than ever before. 'Seig Fucken Heil' ruled and being fearless and feared earned you respect. There were two things the prisoners didn't tolerate inside and that was child molesters - 'kid fuckers' as they were know colloquially - and narks. Serious physical damage was always just around the corner for these men the minute a shaft of light opened up in their security. As a result they were often taken out of play and placed in high security seclusion away from other inmates or they were killed. The inmate's code made damn sure you remained a silent spectator; you had little alternative but to turn a blind eye to these incidents. These were the sorts of things that commonly happened inside and your indifferent reaction to it all just became second nature. Reprisals from old unresolved scores, both inside and outside the cage, meant you had to watch your back constantly.

Different gang groups in the prison were allocated to separate blocks to control the risk of conflict between rivals. We were situated in B Block while D Block was the high security section. On this lag I found myself in D Block, the heaviest security section within the prison. Spitting on the walls of the corridors and cells to make the place more ugly than it was became emblematic of where my heart and my very being was at. My rebellion against any form of authority became more and more pronounced. My mind was firmly gripped by mongrelism now; there was no way I was going to listen to anyone or anything I didn't believe in unless it was Mob related. And even that was tested. I rebelled against the screws and threw food in their faces. I was put on report and classified as high risk. I was then placed in isolation and segregated from other prisoners while I was in D Block. The cells here had double doors and I was strip-searched regularly. I was locked down twenty-four hours seven days a week, with one hour per day out of the cell in the yard, which included fifteen minutes for a shower. All alone I created an exercise routine to keep my body physically fit and coupled this with the discipline of keeping my cell clean. Isolation gave you a lot of time to think, but in a subconscious balancing act I became afraid to think too much lest I drift into depression. I often thought nostalgically about the food that I could eat outside like the pineapple drinks I could sip from the Wairoa fish'n'chip shop. Other times I'd conjure up the dog inside me to feed my hate for the world. I wanted to survive this experience and take out my loathing on the world. I was allowed to read books including pornography, which allowed me to relieve a build-up of sexual tension, and sometimes I was allowed to do certain hobbies.

In maximum security for so long you learned the routine and how to get along with the other guys from other gangs, many of whom became great friends over time. There was a comradeship that developed amongst the inmates here that sometimes went beyond my Mob thinking about comradeship. The brothers inside needed to unite if they were to survive within and beyond these walls of confinement. The Paremoremo comrades aptly named the 'Parry Comrades' was an entity created inside the prison to cater for the need to unite all those who did time here.

This brotherhood was represented by the insignia of two fists linked by a broken chain in the middle. The fists stood for the prison comradeship between gang members, criminals and lifers, while the broken chain represented the idea that while you lived in a prison no authority ultimately ruled you, each was free within that brotherhood. Many of the guys tattooed this image on our bodies, while others did not affiliate themselves with this symbolism at all. All were welcome to join this team of guys as long as you were in Paremoremo Prison. All were linked-up by the talisman of whanau under the 'Parry Comrade' emblem. This was true for both those who recognised this while in prison and for those who'd been released to the outside world. For those who joined, you would always be brothers no matter what happened or where life would take you.

Many of the Mobsters inside were vehemently opposed to this kind of solidarity - as far as they were concerned the Mob ruled and that was that. I did not support the 'Parry Comrades'; I had my own team to hang out with. In response to the creation of the 'Parry Comrades' and the sheer numbers of guys entering these four walls, we created the Mongrel Mob Paremoremo chapter with its own bulldog design - a front view of a bulldog with no helmet. The name Mongrel Mob was on the top rocker rim while Paremoremo lined the bottom rocker. It was a revolutionary piece of artistry and invention and in a small way an historic occasion:

we were the first to create a new gang chapter within a prison system in New Zealand. We unified the Mob brothers inside from different chapters under this new entity. This idea caught on at other prisons. We quickly grasped the need to create power within the prison to protect the mana and image of the Mongrel Mob both inside and outside the prison walls. In my time there Kinch - an ex-army man with great leadership skills - was elected Paremoremo Mongrel Mob president.

For years the Kingpin system ruled the jail, where an inmate, who proved to be the toughest guy in the prison, both physically and mentally, ruled the roost. However, when large numbers of gang members began to come through the prisons the Kingpin was at first isolated and then overpowered and overruled by the Mobsters. The Kingpin system was neutered and remained unrecognised by our boys because it was always at the mercy of too many challengers. The gangs were now too strong and eventually the strongest gang leaders inside replaced the Kingpin system. If the Mongrel Mob were strong inside it was the Mob presidents that became the so-called Kingpins, while the old Kingpins allied themselves with other gang factions. There was a continuous power play in the prison where the ruling gang presidents of the time had a special relationship with the screws who soon recognised the power these men had with other inmates. Creating a working relationship with the gang leaders allowed the screws to run the prisoners with little friction. This was where I witnessed the enormity and power of the Mongrel Mob both inside and outside the prison, simply because of the sheer numbers of guys arriving in the prison.

Many guys entered prison from other Mob chapters and they came under the united authority of the Paremoremo chapter. And, what was happening outside the walls affected the reputation of the gang on the inside. If an opposing gang were to take out members of the Mob and their whanau in a district where they were not strong, we would take it out on the opposing gang members who were sitting in jail.

I remember a Polynesian brother, a big strong body-builder, who harassed our young guys inside. He was semi-patched with the Mongrel Mob but wasn't truly committed to us. Many of the Polynesian boys were patched up under our gang and we tried to find a way to teach this big guy a strong lesson. We invited him to have a drink with us. We made our own homebrew, which we offered him after we had spiked it with antidepressants - medication from some of the boys who didn't swallow it. After drinking the spiked elixir the Polynesian brother walked into the prison movie theatre only to emerge later obviously affected by our concoction. This gave us the chance to give him the bash for his behaviour towards our young prospects. He had to be removed to another block for his own protection.

Often new brothers coming into jail would take out their frustration on other guys in the jail, which could cause relationship problems for us. We knew the parameters of hierarchy and relationship between the rival gangs in prison and that had to be protected. When problems arose between 'newbies' and other prison factions, we had to step in and take both an authoritative and protective role with our own guys. Any angry grudges guys held could be taken out on someone on the rugby field particularly when our own 'crash team' (rugby team) played against other blocks. These games were unselfconsciously designed to allow the boys to let off steam like they were old railways rolling stock.

The sheer number of Mobsters who entered the prison for crimes such as rape and murder changed the face of the way the culture ran within the prison. While our authority created long-standing relationships with other factions in the prison in a bid to sustain a balance, each faction still had to control its own people. This unusual comradeship meant brothers stood up for each other when there was a sniff of unfair play. Even if the screws acted against certain inmates in the wrong, it was nothing for us to smack them over to save a brother. In various ways the screws had to be careful how they manhandled us in case they initiated an utu situation that once set in motion had to be exacted.

Socially, my best friends inside were the brothers I originally went to prison with, including my old time ally, Porky. We ate, worked, and did our lags together; we even joined the prison kapahaka (traditional Maori dance) team under the leadership of kuia Ann Tia where we performed concerts for the prisoners and visitors.

Visits from family were frequent but I really wasn't particularly interested. I just wanted the gifts and food they brought me, that's all. Occasionally religious prison ministry groups would preach to us about the Bible and God, but it was like pouring liquid into a bottomless pit in the hope it would form a lake. It didn't register with me at all. What was all that crap they spat out about a loving God? What was love? No one showed love here, it was frowned upon. I couldn't even recognise the word 'love' let alone work out what it meant. It was a word without meaning so to hit me with the idea of a loving God and what he had done for me was detestable. Give me the bash! That was the love I knew.

This was the world I was to experience while in prison for three years and nine months. There were both highs and lows in prison, but the lows seemed to preoccupy my mind constantly. I learned to fight and defend myself, my knowledge of boxing playing a large part in defending my life. I also learned to comfort myself mentally and emotionally because no one else was going to do it for you. In the lonely times I threw myself into the hobbies and craftworks the establishment provided. I was also diagnosed as psychotic, mentally ill and suicidal. I would often hear the spirits of ancestors talking or crying in the cells, their images appearing in my breath on cold days. These were either the spirits of ancestors who lurked in my own background, or they were those of Maori ancestors buried in the landscape and swamplands the prison was built on. I was placed on sleeping pills and antidepressants to help my emotional state. Life wasn't a bed of roses inside; it was hard, painful and often emotionally damaging. However, at the same time it was also characterised by brotherhood and solidarity.

Chapter Six
ON THE RAMPAGE

In 1979 I was released from Paremoremo. I was troubled and rebellious, and I felt the world owed me big time. Not only that but I had to make up for a lot of lost time. As far as I was concerned 'justice sucked' - a phrase many guys tattooed on their foreheads. An escort van transported me from Paremoremo to Albany where it had been organised for me to meet up with the Mongrels from the Auckland chapter. Exiting the vehicle I kicked the hub of the prison van and yelled at the big Dutch warden to 'Fuck off'. He replied with the old screw cliché delivered in a revealing and prophetic tone: 'You'll be back.' Meeting up with the Auckland brothers in their Mark II Zephyr was a great relief. Being let out of jail was usually accompanied with the traditional Mob 'root, rumble and rage'. The guys drove me straight to the pub where women, booze and a rumble were organised and made available to me.

The rebellion inside of me was ripe and the guys I was camped with had to put up with my unruly ways. They didn't really know how to handle me and sometimes copped the brunt of my rebellion against the system. I was on alcohol, pills or anything I could stuff down my throat to get out of it. These liquorice allsorts drug concoctions became a form of escapism from life. Eventually I became integrated back into the normality of Mob life on the outside. Returning to the real world I saw a lot of changes in the Mob. New chapters had emerged: the Papakura Rogues who had no fixed abode, the Notorious chapter based at Mangere, and the Auckland chapter from Mangere and Grey Lynn. The old original chapters from Hastings, Wellington, Manawatu, Porirua, Napier, Wairoa, Gisborne, Taumarunui, and Tauranga were still humming along. There were a lot of new guys in the gangs now, guys I didn't know. The dress code had changed but the mentality was much the same. Probably the one thing I noticed was that the level of debauchery in the gangs had soared out of control over the years.

I spent six weeks with the Auckland Mongrel Mob Chapter who eventually transported me back to Taumarunui to my home King Country chapter. The first port of call in town was the pub, where I was met by Fatso. The boys stood around me to make sure I was all right. They assimilated me back into the chapter with a drink and I came back under the leadership of the current president Disco Duck, and Crossy, the vice-president. Reunited with my home chapter meant it was their responsibility to protect and look after me. The brothers all shared their aroha (love) with me in various ways to welcome me home.

The Christmas of 1979 and the New Year for 1980 was spent in Northland with the current vice-president's family. I had never been up north and so two carloads of us journeyed to Kaikohe in Mk II and MK III Ford Zephyrs. All the way north we were intoxicated and we had to pinch petrol to fill our vehicles. Wearing our patches and flying our Mongrel

Mob colours in Northland offended the Black Power gang. This was their turf. When we entered the Kaikohe pub the word got around pretty quick a pack of Mongrels were in town. It was almost inevitable we would meet and rumble. A troupe of Black Power guys from Whangarei soon arrived to teach us a lesson about trespassing on their territory. While they were busy drafting and organising their men, we made an attempt to find some form of weaponry. We had nothing on us but we found someone in Moerewa who helped create Molotov cocktails - petrol bombs. While there I met Pumpkin, an old Rangipo prison network mate, who supported us. He provided us with psychological support, marijuana and women. We also rang up for support from Taumarunui, and in no time a car full of King Country brothers arrived on the scene. We celebrated our visit to Moerewa with a sex orgy down at the river with Pumpkin's young women. While we frolicked naked in the paddock we saw the Black Power pass through Moerewa, on their way north to combine with their forces in Kaikohe. After our loins had rested we eventually made our way to Kaikohe, with our petrol bombs at the ready to confront the Blacks. Arriving in town, the Black Power had gathered their forces near the top pub at the other end of town and as we drove past them we made taunting gestures to provoke the first move. In the end we never had to use the cocktails and there was no rumble, no fight, no injury. No-one won on that day and it just ended as a stand-off, a show of power that found itself channeled through an emasculated litany of taunts. In the end everyone just retreated from what ended up as a phony war.

I had only been out of jail for six weeks when I found myself under arrest again for the assault of a woman in Kaikohe. I was arrested in Kaikohe and sent to Mt Eden Prison again on remand. Bail was set and the Auckland guys once again saved my bacon by putting up the money for my bail. This time I just absconded and didn't turn up to court on the posted date. I had instead decided to go on the run. I hid in the arms of the other Mob chapters and with family members who weren't aware I was actually on the run. I made my way to the old stomping grounds at Taumarunui but eventually drifted down to Christchurch where there was a Mongrel Mob convention in progress. These gatherings were usually three days of companionship doused in parties, women and booze. On the third day the presidents would meet and deliberate on the plans for future conventions. At the end of this gathering I stayed in Christchurch to continue my worship of booze and the guitar. I was so rebellious at this point in my life that I even defied the Christchurch president's commands. I just wouldn't listen and caused more trouble than I was worth. Later I heard straws were drawn as to who would be chosen to assassinate me.

Knowing I had outstayed my welcome in the south, I hitched back to Wellington where I stole a car to travel up to Palmerston North. The car ran out of gas in the Manawatu where I was eventually picked up by the police and placed in Manawatu Prison at Linton. A backlog of charges were thrown at me: absconding from probation; absconding from bail; stealing; car conversion; and assault on a woman I had urinated on. Sitting in my cell, I contemplated the stories I had heard while on the run of Mob guys I knew from home committing suicide. The circumstances of their lives had become unbearable and they chose death - I felt I was moving in the same direction. I soaked up the news of their actions but becoming consumed by the aroha and brotherhood of their lives I was plunged into a great sadness. Tying the bed sheets around my neck I tried to thread the end through the roof beams to lynch myself. The urge in me was so strong I wanted to be true whanau to those guys by following in their footsteps. Life in this world didn't mean anything to me anymore, or so it seemed. I tried to tighten the noose around my neck but every time it failed to grip.

My criminal reputation was now growing amongst the Mob at the same time as the law had identified me as a dangerous criminal in the eyes of the public. I was now a marked man in more ways than one.

In 1980 I was sent to Mt Eden Prison for twelve months. It was a medium risk prison and once again ruled by the Mongrel Mob. I was quite at home here with the brothers I knew. Many rumbles used to take place inside the walls. If we got wind of altercations against our brothers on the outside we would take out retribution on members of rival gangs who were doing time in Mt Eden.

Confrontation with our boys was met with immediate and stern retribution, even if that meant one-on-one combat. This upheld the mana of the gang inside. During an inter-block rugby game I witnessed some harsh treatment towards a few of our young prospects so I stepped in and roughed up a couple of guys on the opposing team. The leaders of the rival gangs on the outside heard through the grapevine what had occurred in this rugby match and ordered their man inside to take me out. He just happened to be the guy I took my anger out on in the game. After I got wind of this challenge I took it head on and in my arrogance I named the place and time for the confrontation. After lock-down our cell doors were secretly opened and we both met in the toilets. When we began to fight my opponent pulled out a long blade knife, but I was hard enough and had enough presence of mind not to flinch. We fought and settled our differences. I still pass by this brother but I hold no animosity against him.

Once a fight was fought all rivalry between factions was extinguished. Everyone knew that.

The screws were helpless to stop this behaviour. In fact the prison officers had to give me further privileges to keep everything inside running smoothly. It was the same deal here as it was in Paremoremo. Living like this in prison I learned quickly to think things out properly and to have some wisdom about decisions, the management of the boys and the appropriate retaliation and retribution if the mana of the Mob was compromised. This meant mulling over all the consequences including the reactions of the screws and the other gangs inside. I had to sort out whether the action was really worth it or not.

Visits from my sister were always interesting. She was a long-standing holy roller, a believer in Jesus Christ of the Bible and she was always preaching to me. At the time I thought she was another version of the crazy Bible-bashing ministers who insinuated themselves into the jails. All that 'God stuff' was a lot of bullshit; to me it wasn't even worth listening to let alone accepting as truth. I often wondered why she even came to visit me considering that the things I had done would have been totally abhorrent to a good Christian woman like her, to her God and to our whanau. Nevertheless, she was always there when she said she would be which I must say I respected. She never gave up on me.

On one visit she gave me a small Bible as big as my hand to keep and read which, I thought at the time, I wasn't about to do in a hurry. Basically, I took it as a gift with no intention of ever reading it. Having left it on my desk in my cell I was caught red-handed with it one day just as I tried to hide it. Usually the brothers would consider you weak having a Bible in your cell, but Pup, the young brother who busted me with it, surprised me when he told me to leave it on my desk. 'It's Okay Bruno you don't have to be embarrassed, leave it there,' he said to alleviate any embarrassment. Little did I know it at the time, but one day the God that my sister believed in would impact my life forever. My mum would also visit me sometimes but my father never ever arrived. Despite every shameful and heinous crime I had committed my mum and sister always said they still loved me; they never denied me the bosom of the family.

Released from Mt Eden I was once again hosted by the Auckland chapters until Porky was released from his prison term in Paremoremo. In the meantime the local Auckland chapters asked me to be their spokesman, as they considered me to be someone with the skill-set they needed to further their cause. I couldn't see why they wanted me to be their spokesman and I thought I lacked the confidence to carry out the role. Gang rivalries were rising in the city with old grudges coming to the fore and territorial disputes becoming a problem. Usually a chapter took over its turf, announced its territorial boundaries and defended it to the death. The Mob's reputation on the outside was marred by shoot-outs with the Black Power and other gangs considered enemies. And, to compound the situation, we were losing numbers. My job was to troubleshoot between warring factions and help rejuvenate gang recruitment. The guys trusted me to help out and put some order into their lives.

It was an interesting situation: the Mongrel Mob chapters - the Rogues, Notorious and others - were full of youngsters, none of whom I really knew. They lacked leaders of my age and sought anyone as a role model to follow. I just happened to be the man they saw as a role model. I was still only a patched member of the Mongrel Mob with no leadership role at all, but these brothers looked up to me despite my pretty uncouth behaviour. I worked for these guys until Porky was released from prison in mid-1982. He picked me up and we returned to the King Country. Porky was like a father figure to me. Our time in prison had made us more than brothers. As far as he was concerned we had done our time in prison and it was time to return home. Arriving back in Taumarunui Porky took over the reins of the gang again; he had the mana to keep us all together and to reunite us as a chapter, despite the many years away.

He got us working back in the community, participating in rugby games or performing with the local kapahaka group. But for some the reality was that they'd rather drink than turn up to practices. Under Porky's rule we attended many tangihanga. He was very comfortable in the Maori world on the marae, but this was not necessarily true for the rest of us. We were fish-out-of-water in that Maori world and it meant little to us. I remember travelling to Opononi in Northland with Porky to pay our respects at the tangihanga of Lobo, a Storm Trooper member who had recently passed away. Lobo was a well-loved member of the Parry Comrades and he had the power to unify prisoners in Paremoremo. He was very protective of the young guys in Paremoremo who'd been dealt a bum deal at the hands of the screws or the dangerous and vicious lifers. He was respected and loved by all the gang members inside. We got to know him well; we'd worked together in the prison workshop sewing up mailbags and that's why Porky was adamant we should show up at his funeral. Paying your respects and showing your face at hui like this was a very Maori thing to do and cemented your mana amongst the people that really counted. It was Porky's nature to show sympathy and aroha in a very Maori way to the whanau of his brothers-in-arms.

This behaviour was unusual. Showing any form of compassion or sympathy for the dead or for the mourning family was a foreign emotion for most of us. Our natural Mongrel attitude was to ignore these emotions; it was not considered cool for a dog to act in that manner. To oppose sympathy and compassion was the norm for us; dead brothers would be honoured by urinating and defecating on or in the coffin. That was the way of a real dog.

Lobo's tangihanga was interesting. When we arrived at the marae there were hundreds of members from rival gangs there to pay their respects. Even though we had scores to settle with some of these guys, Porky put all animosity to one side on this occasion. He walked straight onto the marae, paid his respects, greeted all the attending gang members, sympathised with the mourning whanau and generally made his presence known. For me this was strange and disorienting as my mind was more interested in picking a fight. But, there was no utu in the air that day.

Porky was certainly a different kettle-of-fish. He was to my mind a great leader: staunch, with no fear of any man, he could walk into any situation and know exactly what to do. He was fair, very giving and held to a vision that pursued a desire to see his boys participate in all facets of community life. He was different to many of the other leaders I knew and had a real sense of whanaungatanga (family relationship) and a considerable knowledge of the reo and local Maori tikanga.

One day the newly formed Te Kuiti chapter turned up to seek acceptance from the Taumarunui chapter while Porky was at the helm. The usual stepping-out of the president failed to happen and their acceptance was actioned with a simple nod from our vice-president. The guys in this chapter were all hard working strong men, shearers and farming types. A very tough and loyal bunch, they were generous to boot with their booze, money and parties. For those of us back from prison it was a time to chill out from our lags; we always had a bottle of booze in one hand and a joint in the other.

The chapter's reputation was put to the test and challenged when a visiting gang filed into the Owhango Hotel without seeking our permission. Most gangs coming through town had to pay homage to the local gang in some way and if they didn't there was always trouble. The prospects would continually be on the look out for visiting gangs on our turf they could start a rumble with. It was at the whim of the president whether anyone took any action or not. On this occasion our president decided to pick a fight. Because this hotel was considered one of our watering holes, and no acknowledgment was made to the King Country Mongrel Mob, Porky kicked over their bikes parked outside to provoke a fight. Inevitably, the bikies stormed outside and met us head on. A huge rumble took place and in the melee Porky was stabbed close to his heart. Later in the hospital the police tried to get information from Porky on the incident to help identify the culprits, but he gave them nothing and neither did we. Narking was something we shunned and to do so was to carry the mark of death.

Porky recovered well from this battle and life sauntered along as normal as life in the Mob could be. Any brush with death boosted your reputation especially if visible scars from your skirmishes could be seen. Your battle stories were remembered and passed on from one member to another, from one generation to another. There was one occasion I remember with Porky that really unsettled me. As we ambled around the town streets with Porky one day it was as though he was taking a final walk around his turf. It was so unnerving and different it was almost spooky. As I followed and watched his interaction with the people and the surrounding landscape I felt a deep ache in my throat as if I was going to lose this brother in my life. It was a thought I didn't want to believe so I pushed it out of my mind. Little did I realise this moment was to be a portent of a drastic change in my life and that of our chapter.

True Red

Chapter Seven
TAKING THE RAP

The week before Easter 1983 while drinking in a bar Fatso, one of the senior Mob members, walked in and told us that Porky had died. He'd passed away in hospital after a heart attack during a kapahaka practice. We firmly believed the previous stab wound he had received at the Owhango Hotel rumble had weakened his heart. As gang members we just continued drinking. What else was there for us to do but drink to our leader's life? Porky's death was to have a profound effect on the chapter, he was no longer there for us and there was now a cloud of vulnerability hovering over a leaderless chapter. All that was left to do was to sing that signature song:

Mongrel Mob memories no one can steal,

Your death left a wound that no one could heal,

Some may forget now that you are gone,

But the Mob will remember, no matter how long.

We were told his body would be ready at 10am on Friday morning for us to claim. All the Mongrel Mob flags were set at half-mast as our red and black Ford Fairlane vehicles arrived at the funeral parlour to pick up the body. Many other chapters attended his final journey through town. He was afforded a president's farewell parade, not a poroporoaki (Maori farewell ceremony), and we drove Porky's body down the main street of Taumarunui and past his favourite haunt, the local pub. He was eventually taken to the whanau's marae at Kaitupeka where he lay in state in Maori fashion for the three day tangihanga. We never disrespected his body.

We made sure our young prospects supported the local marae people to prepare food and ensure the marae was set up to receive the manuhiri (visitors) that would come to pay their respects. Meanwhile, many of us returned to the pub to drown our sorrows in jugs of alcohol as that was our protocol and the only way we knew how to mourn. Mongrel Mob chapters from Porirua, Wellington, Manawatu, Hastings, Napier, Gisborne, and Auckland all arrived to attend the tangi and pay their respects to the life of a courageous Mob leader.

These visiting gang members eventually met us at the pub where we consumed gallons of alcohol as our signature of mourning. One thing Porky wouldn't have wanted was for us to sit around his tupapaku (dead body) and mourn his death all day long. He would have wanted us to continue with life and enjoy ourselves. I played the party game celebrating the memory of Porky's life with a jug of beer - no level of emotion was ever acceptable amongst the ranks, that was a sure sign of weakness. In reality the death of my mentor, my brother and my friend had left a huge gaping hole in my heart that no amount of alcohol could fill or heal. The ache in my throat had returned and just like the others I pulled down the staunch and unemotional Darth Vader mask, yet inside me a river of tears was flowing like a raging waterfall. I was unable to express my grief for his loss in a public way, due to the code of the Mob. Once again I was predictably lost and lonely.

After six hours solid drinking in honour of Porky's death, an invitation was made for everyone to attend a battens up/disco fundraiser at one of the other local marae. At the fundraiser I was isolated as being a bit hoha (a pest) and a local nuisance. On a couple of occasions I was asked to leave, didn't listen and carried on being a mischievous drunk. At around 1am the disco shut down and I returned home in my V8 Chev Impala 287. I was unaware that some of the Mobsters who attended the fundraiser had kidnapped and pack-raped a young teenage woman down at the river sometime between 11pm and 1am that morning. Around 8am the next morning a carload of police officers and a detective-sergeant knocked on my door and arrested me for alleged rape. I was still drunk and grieving the death of my leader. I denied the charge but didn't put up any resistance. All I knew was I had nothing to do with this incident but it was to be the beginning of a fourteen month battle to prove my innocence.

I was placed on remand at Waikeria Prison for nine months. I had a lot of time to think about the circumstances of my life. How did I go wrong and end up in this mess? All I wanted at this point was freedom. Maybe these ruminations were a wake-up call, but at the time I couldn't see it clearly. I was lost as to how to change and how to get myself out of the quicksand that always seemed to be sucking me down. I felt like I had been kicked in the guts, life seemed hopeless. In all this the memory of Porky was constantly on my mind, how would I survive without him?

On remand I was forbidden to work. Every day I was locked up from 3.30pm in the evening till the next morning at 7.30am when I was released for breakfast. From 9am till 11am I was released into the yard until 11am when I was locked up again in my cell. From 1pm to 3.30pm I was given another period of free time in the yard. Every spare minute I had I would run, exercise, play touch football or train on the weights to maintain my fitness - that kept me sane. As a mobster I was big and heavy, mean looking, wearing toe-capped boots always. But here I lost a lot of weight. I became ruthlessly fit and my body was athletically toned.

I met another Maori guy while on remand who discretely told me about his son who was in the Black Power. That kind of an admission in front of my fellow Mobsters would usually have seen this man given the bash. Instead of lashing out I claimed this man and his son as my brothers under my protection. Ten years on I would meet that man's Black Power son under very different circumstances.

I remember a pipe that ran along the back wall of my cell into every other cell on my wing. Some guy would constantly tap out tunes on that pipe for entertainment, the noise resonating through all our cells. While it was this guys' way to pass the time of day for many of us it was annoying and disturbed our concentration. He was identified as the culprit in the yard and given the bash. That was life inside.

My case eventually went to trial in the Hamilton High Court. I was found guilty and sentenced to six years imprisonment to be served at Mt Eden Prison in Auckland. I remember being not only devastated by the decision but totally defenseless - there was nothing I could do. I even toyed with the idea, in a fever stoked by injustice, that my own lawyer had misrepresented me.

Being back in the cells at Mt Eden to begin my lag left a bitter taste in my mouth. It was like I was in a state of utter despair and I felt my life had been destroyed because of a witness's wrong identification. A large number of the inmates were Mobsters, all guilty of their crimes. But, I knew I was wrongly accused and had taken the rap because it was considered cool in the Mob to suck it up and, having staunchly copped it, heighten your Mob reputation. But deep down my sense of justice had been vanquished and it tore at my heart. Then I began to spout off that I was innocent of the charges and while the brothers inside were sympathetic others just said: 'Harden up and get on with your lag, bro!' I was placed in a separate single cell I was to make my home. Brothers in Paremoremo sent messages expressing the hope I'd get transferred back there to the hub of the lifers and in the state I was in I sure as hell wasn't looking forward to staying here for too long if I could help it.

The usual routine of waking up in the morning, picking up breakfast in the dining hall and returning to my cell to eat was to be my lot. In the yard we were able to mix with the others. I spent my time in prison training to keep my body and mind fit and my anger fueled. My relationship with some of the prisoners became one of sympathy especially amongst those who knew I was innocent. I earned a reputation both in and out of the prison for taking the rap for a crime I didn't do. In the eyes of the Mob I was 'staunch' for doing someone else's time and it was a label of distinction you wore, like a military decoration for bravery, all your life. Being a Mongrel and doing a lag in prison gave you a certain status, a bit higher than the normal criminal. The label of 'staunch' may have consoled me momentarily but it was a verbal ointment that didn't really soothe the pain in my heart.

After a few weeks I was elected president of the new Mt Eden Prison chapter we'd created. Artists drew up a Mt Eden Prison Mongrel Mob symbol, a bulldog on its side with no helmet, and everyone had it tattooed on their bodies. The favoured position for this insignia was on the right shoulder in memory of the very first Mobster's swastikas that were worn there. I endorsed this re-branding and it happened to coincide with an initiation hand-over to me, as president, of the Mongrel Mob diary. This diary was an account book of all sales of smokes, drugs and chocolate both in and out of prison. In prison chocolate bars replaced money and a large drug trade thrived using chocolate. No names were ever written in this book and the chocolates acted as our cash substitute inside. We sold out hundreds of raffles using chocolate bars and the numbers were placed in a hat and drawn-out by the screws. The winners received coffee tables with paua (abalone shell) inserts, glass paintings, leather crafts or carved lamp stands. We also had cash and chocolates smuggled inside to fuel our gambling schools.

As president it was my responsibility to maintain the mana of the dog within the prison walls and to ensure the code of the Mob ruled: ripping off anyone and everyone who wasn't Mongrel Mob and bribing and dealing to the screws. I created an amicable relationship with the prison officers and I got to know them well at the same time as they became pretty conversant with my personality. The screws were smart enough to know if we worked together I could make their job a lot easier.

I began to think deeply about my life, my association with the Mob and my future. Mob life began to seem utterly futile. Were we to continue living a day-by-day life of inferiority without a vision for the future and a sense of hope, and to continue wasting vast amounts of time in prison? My mind was in a state of turmoil tossing around the possibilities of a positive future instead of constantly indulging the negative in a round of being drunk every day, partying, being on the run, courting arrest, and being judged, sentenced and imprisoned. The Mob mentality could be summed up by the notion that the more positive your mind the more unworthy of the bulldog you were. Conversely, the more negative and antisocial you were the more your reputation remained firm. I pondered how we as an organisation could ever become successful in the future. If we held onto our old consciousness, caged in a prison of our own minds, we would never be able to find a pathway for creative new ideas. Put simply I asked myself: 'What the hell am I doing in a prison for a crime I never committed?'

Five months into my six year sentence, I was handed the right to an appeal through the law society who found me a lawyer who could help. My appeal was upheld on the grounds of misidentification and the evidential fact that I was never at the location when the incident occurred. A retrial was set in the Wellington High Court for March 1985 and I was out on $5000 bail the Mob raised. Released, I walked out of the prison past the cells of my brothers as they filled their cell buckets with water and threw them over me. This was the brothers' farewell for a comrade, a sort of Mob baptism into life outside the walls. Dripping wet, I saluted the guys in my own quiet way. I was humbled to feel the support from the guys at that moment; we were brothers indeed. It remains an emotional moment in my life to this day.

I was told to report to the court and stay out of trouble for the next five months. I stayed with my brother in Otara who, at the time, couldn't have cared less what happened to me. I had a gardening job in South Auckland for a period until I was able to find my way down to the retrial in Wellington. I made my way back to Taumarunui and after a meeting with the vice-president we decided to make a detour to Gisborne to find witnesses who could plead my innocence. My car was chocker with guns ready to retaliate if there was any reluctance to proving my innocence. However, in Gisborne there was no opposition and a witness agreed to testify in court and to tell the truth. Arriving in Wellington, Mob members from Porirua, Gisborne and the King Country came to support my case. After a two day trial, the jury retired to deliberate on my appeal. I was locked up downstairs considering my life while upstairs the jury considered the facts. What I was grimly staring at was a twelve year sentence if I lost. At that time I knew I would have to just bite the bullet if the whole thing turned septic. When the jury arrived back in court after an hour, I was called to the dock to answer a few more questions. Five hours later the jury announced their verdict: not guilty of rape on the grounds of misidentification. The victim was well known to us and she knew me well. Raped by outsiders she could not remember or recognize, she fingered me because I was the same build as one of the other guys. Even my brother co-offender who was sentenced with me gave evidence that I was not there at the time. Additionally, three other witnesses saw me at the marae at the time of the rape. Strangely, the first lawyer who represented me failed to present this evidence.

Hearing the verdict I was in two minds: relieved I was not guilty but filled with rage and anger at my treatment. I wanted to be compensated for all I had gone through whether that was in the shape of an apology or some form of physical revenge. Repeating a pattern that just seemed to go round and round like a carnival Ferris wheel I found solace in alcohol, the pub and the comradeship of the brothers of the Porirua and Wellington

Chapter Eight
THE PRESIDENCY

Back in Taumarunui my anger festered for days. On the sharp end of rebellion I sent the boys out on booze binges, drug selling, car conversions, robberies and window smashing. Within a week a meeting was held at Oparure Marae at Te Kuiti where the Te Kuiti, Otorohanga and Taumarunui chapters met to discuss the future leadership. Because I'd taken the rap for crimes I didn't do, and had a prison record and leadership qualities I was considered worthy to be nominated as the president of all three chapters. There were some who didn't support my nomination so I confronted these guys face-to-face. They quickly changed their stance and stood up in my favour. The presidency was firmly placed in my hands in 1986.

At our first meeting in Te Kuiti I implemented a number of edicts for the members to adhere to. When I saw many of the guys drinking twenty-four hours a day, seven days a week, I asked myself if these guys would ever straighten up - they were out of control and wasting their lives. While in prison I'd thought long and hard about my own future and the future of the Mongrel Mob. What purpose did it serve drinking ourselves into oblivion, being involved in crime, running from the law, spending all our days in prison and spilling our own blood? This was a snapshot of my own life and many of the other boy's lives, and for my part I didn't want to continue that life forever. I didn't want us to pass on this lifestyle to our children and grandchildren. I wanted a more positive lifestyle for the brothers, where education, work ethic, trade and business were part of our ethos. But I knew this mental realignment would be fraught with problems. After all, the Mob was always about the dog lifestyle and I knew it was going to take a new mental readjustment for the guys to accept this. Personally, I knew that either I implemented some new ethics now or I'd die in a pit of worthlessness. I took steps to encourage the boys to cut back on their drinking in the evenings, to keep our houses clean and to pursue employment initiatives. I also made Sunday a day for all the chapters in our region to meet for a feast to pull all our whanau together. Further, I invited the local people to eat with us. Many of the boys dragged their heels about this but they had to accept the word of the president. I was trying to bring some order to the boy's lives.

Over the next three months I pushed each chapter in the King Country to create their own separate infrastructure that would report to me. The new alignment I instituted as president consisted of a vice-president, sergeant-of-arms, secretary and treasurer. My vice-president was to implement my instructions, instruct and advise and, through a report, indicate to me what was happening with the different chapters.

My sergeant-of-arms held on to my armoury. If I ever needed to go hard out he was on hand to pass on weaponry to me. He carried my own personal .45 Colt pistol. I loved guns but, at the same time, we all knew their dangers. We carried them on our bodies, hid them in our houses and cars, and even slept with them under our pillows. Sometimes the bullets we had didn't even fit the barrels but we didn't care as long as the damned things fired and hurt those we aimed at. Often when I was drunk I would play Russian roulette with people or just indiscriminately fire off my pistol. We also had an array of sawn-off shotguns effective at short range, long barrelled shotguns, unregistered firearms stolen from shops and guns our fathers and grandfathers had brought back from World War I and II. My own .45 came from those war years and belonged to an uncle of one of the guys in the Te Kuiti chapter.

My secretary at this time was an Egyptian brother named George who I'd met in prison. George had been doing time for manslaughter. This cat had great expertise at business strategy and administration. We became great brothers inside so we decided to patch him up with the Mob at Te Kuiti after his release from prison. He was like a square peg in a round hole: sometimes he fitted in with us, other times he didn't just as he knew when to wear his patch and when not to. His job was to establish contracts for our trust and help develop good business enterprises.

My treasurer was in charge of the gang's money and he made regular reports on all income and expenditure. Our income came in from a number of fronts: membership payments (which everyone had to pay no matter how poor you were), drug money, robberies, gifts and donations from other chapters, and government funds from work contracts. In my time we would send our prospects out to sell drugs, mainly marijuana, at a 100% mark-up, and if they didn't return with all the cash they would get the bash. I would personally see to that. The marijuana was brought or traded via guys we had met in prison, guys we could trust. Other times the drugs we purchased to resell came from high-rolling businessmen. Dope had a calming effect on the boys and was openly shared with everyone as long as business kept pumping along. Pounds of weed were sent out to the chapters to sell and when the cash rolled back we were usually raking in around $30,000 a week. This money was deposited into the chapter's bank accounts. There was nothing we didn't have or need to keep the gangs rolling and profitable.

As a president you had to play the part: I had big V8 cars with a chauffeur, drugs, girls, power and authority. I was like a dog on heat - everything was on tap; anything I desired I had.

Eventually I moved my operations to Auckland where there was better work and business opportunities. Here I could be closer to the government funding organisations we needed to forge a relationship with. Another reason for the move was due to the fact that the police in the King Country were always on my case. There was nowhere I could go without the cops hovering close by. I set up the Nga Kuri Rohe Potae Work Trust in Auckland to facilitate employment contracts for the Taumarunui and the other King Country chapters. I was able to run the King Country as well as find employment opportunities for our boys from Auckland. Once we were set up in Auckland it was easy to create an infrastructure in Taumarunui to send funds down from Auckland.

I secured a gorse and privet hedge cutting contract for some of our boys in a location directly opposite from the Black Power pad and that made things interesting. The boys took precautions on the work site - alongside their chainsaws were guns for protection. Some of the brothers working on this job suffered bad asthma and allergy based illnesses due to the association with these noxious weeds. I thought they were simply trying to dodge work and sent them back to work regardless of their sickness. I was never sick in my Mongrel Mob life and as far as I was concerned they shouldn't be sick either - there was no room for illness in the Mob unless you were dying. Sickness was just another sign of weakness.

I'd heard about the housing schemes and other business ventures the Black Power were involved in and this inspired me. I decided to make some enquiries. The Labour Department was able to broker a meeting with Abe, the leader of Mana Mangu Aotearoa (Black Power Aotearoa - South Auckland), to discuss the type of work and income strategies that organisations like ours could take advantage of. Abe and I met at the Labour Department. He turned up in a white limousine and I arrived in my red Ford LTD. Meeting Abe face-to-face was a humbling occasion for me. Black Power and the Mongrel Mob had been at each other's throats for sometime but there was no personal animosity on my behalf. In the early 1970s we all used to drink together in the pubs and there was very little inter-gang hostility. On top of all this, any general antipathy I'd had toward Black Power had dissipated over the years - a process that had come about through prison associations and the development of a bond of brotherhood. I knew Abe was successful in his work operations and had built a great pad for his members and it was a privilege to sit alongside him this day. We were not rivals at the time and I'll always remember his courtesy. He took me on a tour of all his operations, shared his future plans and showed me aerial photos of the Black Power pad. He had an engineering organisation on the go, a Harley Davidson shop, a model housing project at East Tamaki and a village he'd built in Otahuhu for his members and their families. He invited my partner and me to his pad for a visit, an invitation I took up without hesitation. Almost inevitably, some of our boys were a little dubious about this kind of meeting. He treated us well indeed, and as we ate crayfish we were able to discuss combined business opportunities and shun the antipathy of the past with its traditional battles that had poisoned us for years. We spoke of the pitfalls of trying to create positive strategies for our gang communities who were, in many cases, still infected with negative mind-sets. He warned me too of the things to look out for that he'd learned from experience. Because the Mongrel Mob mind-set was a lot more antisocial than Black Power I knew this kind of thinking would need influential support. He treated me like royalty and inspired me to create something along the same lines as Black Power. My vision for a more unified Mob with a cleaner act was in sight; maybe we had stopped looking through the wrong end of the telescope. While no specific deal was made between Abe and myself I maintained a great friendship with him over the next three years. My respect for him remains undiminished and it was a privilege to know that brother.

During these months a Mongrel Mob convention was held in Wairoa, which gave me an opportunity to take my boys from Otorohanga, Te Kuiti and Taumarunui to my home-town to meet my folks. We parked up on the family's front lawn and walked into my family home where my father welcomed us unconditionally and with open arms. I was grateful to my father for his love for me and the boys, and his open-hearted hospitality. He never criticised me or my boys once. As a father he had every right to hang me out to dry but he was always accepting and inclusive in his attitude until the day he died. My father never changed his mind toward the gang and me.

Returning home to the rural papakainga reminded me in many ways why I never wanted to move back there: My life had become firmly entrenched in the fast lane of the cities and the prisons. I couldn't see myself in the rural backblocks even if that meant seeing my whanau regularly. I was also aware there could easily be trouble at the convention and looming was the prospect I could be nabbed for yet another crime I did not commit. I became very conscious of not being somewhere that tied me to a crime and I made sure I arrived in the morning of the convention and left in the afternoon to avoid any potential conflict or confusion. The army and police had surrounded the town expecting trouble; there had been a shoot-out between the Mongrel Mob and the Black Power earlier and the smell of retribution befogged the air like a decaying animal. While I was in Wairoa I made sure I paid special homage to my parents and to all the other leaders who had attended. It was here at the convention that I mooted the idea of holding the next Mongrel Mob convention in Auckland under my own mana and stewardship. A decision was made after I left the convention to honour my request.

It was my mission to create a working relationship with government departments in Auckland for work, but this meant cleaning up our act before we could even entertain receiving any government funding. My guy's work ethics had to be raised if we were to prove we could accomplish the work we were commissioned, while our drug behaviour had to be reigned in if we were to be perceived as anything other than outlaws. To carry this out in the real world would be hard as our previous incarnation had been transient and imbued with entrenched criminal Mobsterism.

We were invited to a rage at the Waikato Mob's celebrations around this time. During the evening, standing outside the premises discussing president's business, a flotilla of motorbikes drove past. As we talked I saw something out of the corner of my eye: a bottle thrown by the bikies hit the Rogue chapter's president, fatally wounding him. We took him to the hospital in a coma but he died a week later. We knew the culprits and a structure was set up by the visiting presidents to instigate a revenge hit. Utu was exacted. For the presidents these kinds of incidents, decisions and orders were a daily occurrence.

As a president, the whanaungatanga or strong family bond with your boys was expressed in a number of ways. Often we sent women to visit the boys in prison to placate their sexual needs and these visits would be organised in part with the leaders inside and in part with the prison screws. On other occasions presents of marijuana and other goods would be sent to the brothers. It was important to reward and honour your brothers, and as a president you became not only their leader but also their protector.

My secretary George mooted the idea of creating a national presidency for the Mongrel Mob. He felt there was a lot of power in numbers throughout the country that could make the Mongrel Mob more than a club, an organisation or a gang; it could become a movement. And a movement needed a national leader. I thought about it and considered it a good idea to chew over with the chapters. I thought the idea should be presented before all the Mob presidents at the Auckland convention and I was inspired to create a meeting with a real difference. As chairman of four gang chapters - Auckland, Rogues, Notorious and King Country - I had to discuss any national presidency structure with these groups first to secure their support before announcing it at the Auckland convention. Because I was too busy organising the convention at this point this discussion was deferred to the Sunday or the last day of the convention.

For the upcoming convention we sought the support of the local mayor, inviting him to a dinner where we all dressed in flash suits and business garb to create the impression we were a trustworthy organisation. He was open to our wishes and finally gave his blessings. We negotiated for a stage, firewood, and access to a park that was big enough to hold a large convention where sports could also be played. We were given permission to hold the convention at Ambury Park despite grumbling from the local ratepayers who were opposed not only to the convention but the location it was to be held. Our team had promised a new look for the Mongrel Mob at this convention and we tried to reassure the local community this was to be a more family oriented movement where even the public were invited to come and picnic, if they dared. I tried to promote a culture of life-change for the Mobsters: we too could become normal citizens where crime and violence didn't have to continually define our public image. We even wore suits to meetings when negotiating with bankers and government department funding agencies. Everyone seemed to accept our word and doors began to open despite some neighbourhood disapproval. I became the personification of the smooth-talking role-player as we exchanged our knives, guns and baseball bats for suits, computers and office equipment.

Money from our community applications began to fill our trust account together with cash gifts and koha from the other chapters. Sometimes real cash would be found mixed with counterfeit dollars. We needed a budget of $20,000 to operate the convention, which we were able to find easily. Preparations for the convention were huge, but we had plenty of brothers to distribute the workload. All the sports, bands and entertainment had been organised and Maori wardens were available for added security. We also had fifteen one hundred gallon mini-tankers of beer on tap. Strictly, women were not allowed to participate in these conventions, but we made sure women were available for the boys if the need was there. We even had one prospect that was given a camera and film and told to take photos of all the convention activities.

To achieve what I thought was an amicable kaupapa for our future I laid down firm rules about any unruly activity: Any chapter who diminished the kaupapa through bad behaviour would reap the consequences, and a moratorium was placed on any form of criminal activity over the weekend. I knew what it was like to take the rap for somebody else's crime and I thought that if I could suck it in so could they. I may have been naive thinking I could control the Mongrel Mob but I was endeavouring to establish some kind of credibility with the public and the local communities we were associated with.

On December 12, 1986, 1000 Mobsters turned up to the Ambury Park convention on the Friday night to the sound of reggae music drifting across the Manukau Harbour. Huge marquees had been erected and all my boys ran security. We had stages in place to welcome all the national brothers, professional bands and a huge bonfire to light up the entire place. This was the first time a Mongrel Mob convention had been projected in this fashion. For accommodation the boys brought their own mattresses or just slept in their cars. I was the only one who had a caravan on the premises.

After a series of negotiations with the politicos we were able to secure an appearance by then Prime Minister Sir Robert Muldoon. We also invited the Minister of Maori Affairs, Koro Wetere to attend but on this occasion he declined. We were disappointed considering 90% of the gang's members were Maori but he did attend subsequent meetings. Muldoon arrived on Saturday morning and was ushered around the park by my secretary to mingle with the boys and to be introduced to the different chapter's presidents. Meeting the prime minister meant we were able to convey our future vision for the organisation. Many of the boys were suspicious of the prime minister and it was a new experience for the gang to have a politician in their midst. Previously, the world of politics had no influence in the gang milieu - we simply didn't care what went on in New Zealand - and our world and mainstream society had never really found a platform on which to meet. However, it was something I felt we should at least try and comprehend if we were to seek government funding in the future.

Playing the host it was my responsibility to put on a good show for the visitors and to remember to pay homage and acknowledge each of the chapter presidents, toasting them with jugs of beer. A number of times I had to stop rumbles between young nuisances but, like it or not, I could see myself in them at that age. I knew I had the charisma and the drive to start this new vision and take it to its limits. Either that or we'd become stuck in a putrid swamp, never to emerge from the excrement dogs love to wallow in. Doing a number of prison terms allowed me to have the drive, discrimination and knowledge to know where not to go, and more importantly, where I didn't want the brothers to go. We were a gang in a state of flux; we were, or so it seemed, a work in progress.

On Sunday morning, my secretary, George, woke me and discreetly shuffled me off the premises and out of Auckland. He'd heard an incident had gone down and he knew immediately that I would have to take the heat. So he saw to it I was not at the park when the police arrived. I was taken to a hotel and told to sit tight. He informed me a rape had gone down during the night that was not sanctioned and it could have huge ramifications for us. The Egyptian didn't want me to become part of the police operation about to happen that morning.

Around 10am roadblocks were quickly placed around the park and over one hundred police cars smothered the whole area. The investigation began and everyone was told to disperse. The local chapter's pads were raided and families were bombarded with force. In the sweep the police eventually arrested Mobsters for all sorts of crimes including those who allegedly raped a young Mangere woman.

I had been told that a group of Mob members had abducted a young eighteen-year-old Maori woman walking her dog through Mangere, smuggled her onto the property and blocked her from Saturday evening to the early hours of Sunday morning. The nine hour ordeal involved rape, beatings, dousing in petrol, violation with a bottle and a torch and urination over her body. She was photographed throughout the ordeal by the young prospect we had given a camera, before she escaped. The photographs became incriminating evidence in a number of arrests. After escaping the ordeal the woman returned with the police and tried to identify her abductors. When a rented vehicle drove away from the Hastings and Wellington chapters encampment, four film cassettes were found that would implicate a number of Mobsters as the rapists. The police investigation would take them on a journey throughout the North Island.[3]

Distracting as this incident was, my initial worry was to ensure that all the hired equipment was returned and the expenses paid or we'd lose all local credibility. The Egyptian became my PR voice while I was out of the loop. I was gutted at the shut down of the convention. Apart from anything else, I was unable to present the kaupapa for a national presidency to all the presidents scheduled for the Sunday afternoon. The second more substantial reason was that my plans and dreams for the Mob were now dismantled and more or less a train wreck. I was shocked and personally I felt I had been set up again. Heaping irony on top of irony I once again felt a sexual incident I had nothing to do with hovered like a malignant ghost and crushed my plans. It felt like I was on trial again. I blamed myself for the incident for not implementing a strategy to cope with a crime of this nature. In hindsight, I should have held pre-talk discussions with all the visiting presidents to outline the rules for the convention to keep it safe. I found out later not all the presidents and their chapters heard the ruling I'd made on the guys behaviour prior to the convention.

I was stupid to think that the Mob mentality could change. I was trying to instill a little bit of positivity into something that had been steeped in negativity since its inception. I asked myself, could it have been any different? Was I that naïve to think I could change things by myself? Could a Mob mentality truly be changed? How could we transform ourselves with an attitude that didn't even recognise going to school, holding down a job or keeping a family as worthwhile? Thinking about it in hindsight I realised the police and justice system, including prison, could not bring any reform to the mongrel world. Instead these agencies fostered a breeding ground for recruitment and our schemes, and an opportunity to pool and refine our criminal skills. I realised too that no societal system was going to change the mentality of the Mongrel mind.

I knew then the Mob didn't care about you as an individual and what you'd been through and I took it personally. The conflict between the entrenched dog mentality and my new diplomacy and world view shattered my heart, like a broken mirror, into a thousand pieces.

The fall-out from Ambury Park developed another awkward twist when I found out that some of the guys at the convention had stolen the big marquee, among other things. I took it as a personal affront and coupled with everything else that had gone down I was now bent on revenge. A series of fierce skirmishes and shoot-outs between my supporters from King Country and the chapter responsible for stealing equipment lasted for six to seven months. To safeguard myself, my house was surrounded with milk bottles to alert us to the approach of anyone at night, guns were hidden in my bedroom and one of my prospects stood sentinel all night. I searched the streets for someone to take a shot at but when the opportunity presented itself the sawn-off shotgun in my hit man's hands would not fire. The target escaped and in my anger I drove to the top of One Tree Hill and pulled the trigger myself. The hammer hit the bullet and exploded into the air. Revenge was never executed on this occasion nor retribution fully paid. I was livid.

Chapter Nine
SURRENDER

'For nine hours last December a young woman was held captive at the site of the Mongrel Mob convention at Ambury Farm Park in South Auckland. She was raped repeatedly, hit and doused with petrol. No Mob members intervened to stop the rape. Many stood and watched, others took pictures. At subsequent police interviews few Mob members showed remorse - most stayed "staunch", loyal to the gang and its code. One asks for a copy of a photo that placed him at the rape scene, for his album, another uses 'Seig Heil' to full stop his sentences at a police interview...'
(The Listener, August 1, 1987).

George the Egyptian took on the job of damage control and told the police and the encroaching and hungry media the gang would hunt down the Ambury Park rapists. He even called for the guys to give themselves up and told them if push came to shove, they'd prefer the legal system to Mob justice.[4] We had declared a moratorium on crime and violence for the convention and George felt it was our duty to assist in finding the culprits and help save face. He reiterated that none of the gang organisers knew what had happened. Precautions had been set up to deter this type of activity and when two women were found on site, whose welfare could have been endangered, they were removed.[5]

George knew this incident could jeopardise the vision we had for the Mongrel Mob. That's why he thought I should now go on a diplomatic shuttle to Hastings to help in the enquiries. This type of diplomacy was foreign to me, but I wanted to support George's diplomatic role. He felt that kind of initiative would show the public we didn't condone the action and we were open to reprimanding our own, we too wanted to move on. I walked into the Hastings police cells and spoke to the brothers on remand, reminding them about the rules that were set down for this convention: There was to be no crime of any form and if any crime was to occur the respective individuals and chapters would have to take responsibility. The boys took my words on board but didn't have too much to say.

What maddened me about the whole affair was that the guys didn't need to pick on an outsider to get their sexual kicks and it put a huge dampener on my vision for the future.

Back in Auckland we made preparations to travel down to Taumarunui to report on the Ambury Park situation. After I gave my opinion and report to the King Country chapters about the handling of the convention and rape aftermath, my leadership was severely questioned. The brothers were not clear on George's role in the whole deal, they disapproved of his comments, they felt his criticism of the Mob had a sharp edge given that most of them did not know him at all. Who the hell was he to be speaking on the Mob's behalf? The guys also questioned my leadership, and my presidency was in serious jeopardy for my perceived mishandling of the situation. Regardless of how the guys felt, I was still the president so to not lose face I decided to confront any issues that had arisen concerning my decisions around the Ambury Park situation by attending a meeting in Hastings with all the Mongrel Mob presidents from throughout New Zealand.

I travelled to Hastings again with Link my vice-president to face all the chapter presidents and we met at one of the local pubs. Questions were asked about my running of the convention, the reason for Muldoon's appearance, the handling of the rape and my motives for the future kaupapa of the gang. I presented my case on the rules I had set up for the convention and admitted that the administration of those rules may have been wanting. I also saw this as an opportunity, misguidedly as it happened, to replay the original idea of a national presidency - an idea originally instigated by George Mamfredos but which I supported. This didn't go down too well. I was also asked why I felt I had to visit the guys in the Hastings cells in public view. In short, they questioned my handling of the whole affair and the meeting fast became steeped in aggravation. I had mud thrown in my face but I stood up and took it. At the meeting's conclusion I lay my patch and presidency down before the other presidents and passed it on to my vice-president, so I would not lose face. I left the meeting without the patch on my back. I felt humiliated and disgusted, a feeling that stoked my anger for many years. Being de-patched was a very serious act in the Mob; I was lucky I didn't get taken out or at least given the bash. If I hadn't surrendered my patch they may have violently taken it from me anyway. And, this wouldn't have been a one-on-one but with the full force of all the presidents' fists and boots. It could have been fatal. I would have expected (and accepted) this course of action but there was enough grace to allow me to exit alive and with some tattered dignity intact.

My ideas for reform and change may've been too visionary then for the guys to understand. Let's face it, it was never going to happen overnight, but at least it made the guys think about their future.

The Ambury Park rape trial saw two of the accused who pleaded not guilty convicted; six others who pleaded guilty were also convicted, while two others were eventually acquitted.[6]

From that day I was a de-patched, naked and lonely man, a stranger amongst my own brotherhood, unaccepted and unrecognised. At least that's how it felt. I returned to Auckland to find George the Egyptian had left - he couldn't help my vision anymore and the situation had become too hot for him to handle. There was no animosity between us on his departure as I recognised his loyalty, his forward thinking and the huge workload he had taken on for me and other Mob members who were associated with him. Undeterred by all this, I tried to continue, backing my own reputation and strength. The agenda I continued to push forward under the auspices of the trust was to modify the Mongrel Mob. As the head of the trust I was still able to secure some Access programmes in mechanics, leatherwork, carpentry, administration and catering through the networks I'd created at the Nga Kuri Rohe Potae Trust.

However, I still had to prove myself to the community and the gangs; I wasn't going to lie down and die like a dead dog. The reality was there were still loyal Mobsters who supported me but conversely I still had a number of detractors. I continued to run the trust from Auckland where many of my staunch patched members from the King Country joined me. The Manukau Urban Maori Authority and Maori Affairs became our

1. Tuhoe 'Bruno' Isaac. (Photograph by Fraser Clements)

2. My father Hondi Isaac. 3. My mother Ngahuia Isaac (nee Hema). 4. Patrick 'Bobo' Tuhoe Isaac - a young boy in Wairoa. 5. In my father's garden behind our house.

6.

6. Firmly ensconced into the Mongrel Mob as 'Bruno'. 7. My King Country Mongrel Mob patch. 8. King Country Mobsters in the early 1980s, Skunk (deceased), Bruno, Porky (deceased) and Pup (deceased). 9. Jinx's tangi, Kaitupeka Marae, Taumarunui, January 1976. (Courtesy of The New Zealand Herald)

10. Porky. 11. Our new style patches. 12. Fully decked out as president in the main street of Taumarunui.

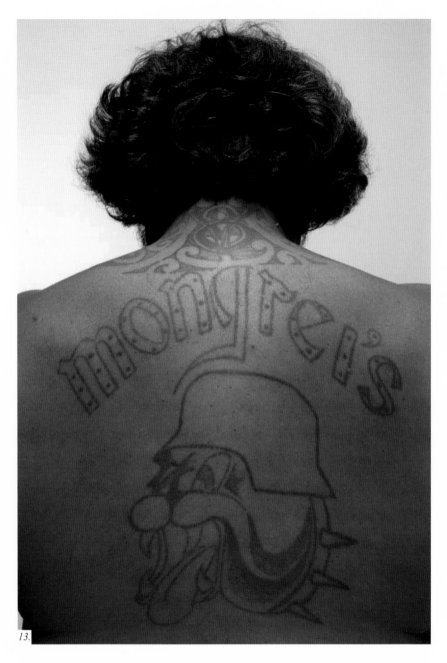

13. The King Country patch tattooed on my back by Porky and others while I was in jail. (Photograph by Fraser Clements).

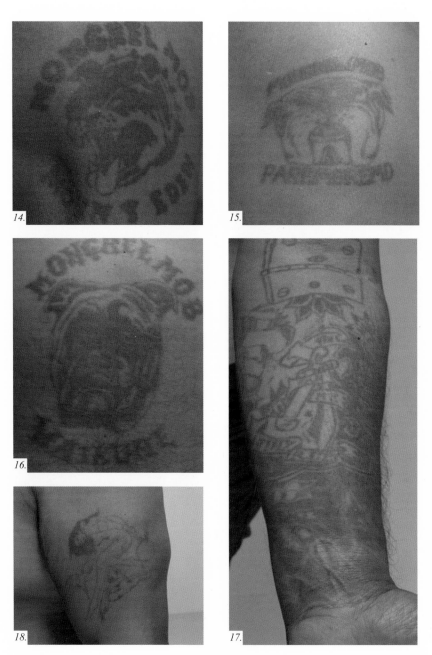

14. Mt Eden Prison emblem. 15. Paremoremo Prison emblem. 16. Waikune Prison emblem. 17. My memorial tattoo to Jinx. 18. Women and skull tattoo. (Photographs by Fraser Clements).

19. George Mamfredos and I fronting local residents prior to the Ambury Park convention. (Courtesy of The New Zealand Herald). 20. At the Ambury Park convention 1986. I am rubbing my eyes.

21. The new me as Tuhoe Isaac with a facial moko. 22. A man on a new mission to reconcile the gangs, October 1997. (Courtesy of the Franklin County News, photo by Dave Hunt). 23. Returning to the funeral of a brother in a transformed state.

24. A modern Tuhoe Isaac. (Courtesy of Arno Gasteiger)

25. On the 'Say No To P' March to Parliament, Wellington. February 2006. (Courtesy of The New Zealand Herald).
26. Tuhoe's Contemplation no. 2. (Photograph by Fraser Clements).

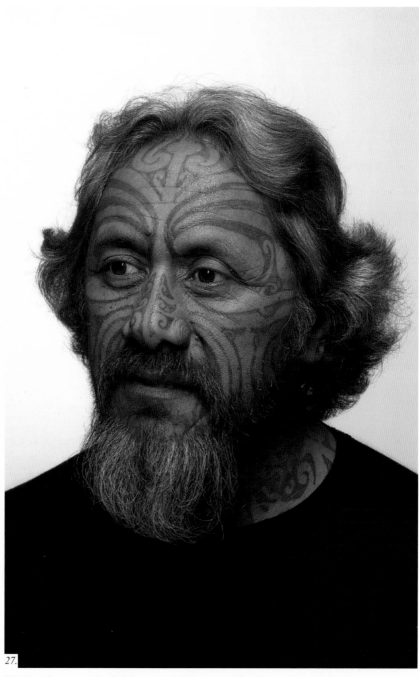

27. A modern portrait of Tuhoe Isaac. (Photograph by Fraser Clements).

umbrella to ensure there was still support for the guys in the gang world intent on some kind of reform. No one was advocating leaving the gang; what we wanted was to be able to earn a living for our families and create a work ethic in the guys. Many of the brothers I knew in prison who had been released entered the programmes we offered. I understood them and tried to help them out for their loyalty to me.

The new vision may have fed my ego and nudged me in another direction but my life was still inextricably bound up with mongrelism; binge drinking, drugs, blocking and unruly behaviour were all as routine as they had ever been. Alcohol began to invade my life to such an extent that I flirted with serious alcoholism. In my mind I was still 'true red' and loyal to the dog mentality. Intellectually I had come to the realisation however that if the Mob was to change then I would have to change, but a big problem circled like a vulture waiting for the hyenas to depart. How could I honestly change, buried as I was, in the world of mongrelism?

Despite my stripped-down status in the gang I still attended later Mob conventions at Dunedin and Wellington, where the leaders had adopted some of the ideas I had blueprinted at Ambury Park. I was given the right to own prospects and eventually I received my patch back from the King Country guys. However, things were never the same from then on and I realised the patch - important as it was to the Mongrels - had little meaning for me now. It had lost its power over me so I burnt it. I found the King Country couldn't feed me anymore, so I laid that connection to rest and left. It was to be the end of an era for me. While my formal Mob allegiance to the dog is no more my loyalty in my heart for the brothers will never die.

During this period of change I tried to adjust to a so called mainstream way of thinking combining this with a Mob world view. I married my partner at the time as we had our first child on the way. I wanted to create an identity that combined a normal family environment with the Mongrel Mob. But the simple idea of mum, dad and the kids, a nice house, a car and a job with the Mob was hard work and sometimes conflicting. While the whanau had all the material things they needed to be happy, there was always tension as I endeavoured to be a husband and a family man at the same time as pushing the business of the Mob.

Fundamentally, I was never home and frequently out of town on Mob business. I had little appreciation of what having a wife and family really meant in this new world I'd created in my head. Realistically, given my consciousness at the time, how could I know what was right when the dog was god in my life - family came last? I didn't know what it meant to head a real whanau distinct from what the ethics of the Mob said it was. I couldn't change despite materially having everything at my fingertips society says you need for a happy life. Happiness and peace hovered on the margins and remained an elusive goal.

While I tried to change the business side of life, the prevailing mindset amongst the guys was completely contrary to the way businesses and trusts were run. I swung between wearing my leathers one day and a suit the next, swapping daily between the gun and the pen. This was not an easy path for many of the guys alongside me as they still saw robbery as their right and their main form of income. Pursuing the work programmes was tricky; the young guys would wander downtown at lunchtime and rob banks and post offices. My Mob sensibility just laughed it off. Carrying on Mob business meant intersecting with the normal practices of drug taking, deals and unsafe sex with prostitutes and Mob women. I was totally ignorant of the dangers of this lifestyle, especially for my wife and child.

One day I saw an advertisement on television that was to change the course of my life. It was about Aids. I was ignorant about Aids or HIV and how lethal it could be not only for me but also for my family. For days I couldn't shake off the lingering images from that advertisement and how devastating Aids could be for the family's future. Looking back, it's interesting how I was never scared of death as a Mobster - a sawn-off shotgun or a knife didn't bother me. In fact I welcomed taunting death like a demented matador - bring it on! - but a bug inside the body scared the hell out of me because it could be passed to the next generation. I didn't care for my own life - I was happy to go to the great bulldog in the sky - I knew little about how to care for my family and the possible contraction of Aids summoned up new emotions that had me by the throat.

I secretly visited the nurse at the doctor's clinic. I'd been there before many times for VD and crabs, but this time I wanted an Aids test. They took a blood test and said the results would not be available for two weeks. There was promotional material highlighting the main points about Aids and to my horror I found out I was complicit in every action that could expose me to Aids - unsafe sex was so normal in my life it was as common as a boil-up. It pulled me up with a jolt and depression set into my very being. The possible consequences I had heaped upon my family hovered in the air like the mediaeval plague and I was breathing it. The next two weeks were the longest weeks of my life. In my mind I thought I was going to my death. And, it was a dark place. Responding in the only way I knew I tried to drown my sorrows with gallons of alcohol and scores of pills. I began to visit people and places I hadn't seen for many years - my old Mongrel Mob haunts - on a final journey before the grave beckoned. I even visited Abe at his pad to have a last drink prior to my final exit. What I didn't do was visit my biological family to inform them of my state; the Mob was my only real family and captive, as I was, to this psychological fever the Mob seemed like the only ones worth visiting.

The day before the test results were due I sat down with my new secretary, told him my situation and handed over the reins of the chapters under my control and the trust to him. I explained how to run the business in the future and gave him the task of looking after my immediate whanau as well. Preparations for my death were now locked in.

When D-day arrived I hadn't slept at all. I finally summoned the gumption to approach my real family - I felt I should go and visit my sister in West Auckland. She was the only link to my real whanau and, more than that, she was the one who always visited me in prison and persisted in preaching God to me. At 6am I knocked on her door in a drunken state. She asked what I wanted coming to her home in a stupour at 6am in the morning. I tried to tell her I was dying of Aids. I explained to her the preparations I wanted for my own funeral. I was to be dressed in my pinstriped suit, the one I'd wear while on trust business, with my King Country patch on my back. Through the lapel buttonhole was to be a red rose. I named only a few guys I wanted to attend the funeral - no whanau were to be there. My favourite AC/DC songs, Highway to Hell and The Jack, were to pump out at my burial ceremony.

I really wanted her to tell me what to do. While I verbally meandered she was blunt and to the point: 'There's only one remedy that can save you if you're serious and that is Doctor Jesus - the great physician.' Being ignorant, naive and totally missing the point I demanded to know when

I could meet him and where his clinic was. She just pointed at a Bible. I hated my sister - she just didn't click with my Mongrel ways - and at this point I loathed her guts for trying to preach to me again. We just didn't connect and we'd never agreed about anything. Her Christianity was always a pain in the neck; it never aligned itself with my Mongrel thinking. It was a load of shit and the people who followed this Jesus character were a bunch of wimps and hypocrites.

At this point I had nowhere else to go and nowhere to hide so I thought: 'What the hell, I've got nothing to lose.' Astonishingly, out of my mouth came the words, 'Yes I do want to meet Dr Jesus.' My sister opened the door preliminary to praying for me. It was a simple message I had heard many times from my sister but it never made sense to me until that moment - that Jesus, the Son of God, died for my crimes, was raised from the dead and now sits at the right hand of God to give us forgiveness, healing and an eternity with God. If I simply believed this and repented of my past God would have mercy on me, heal me and accept me as one of his sons. I had heard all that rubbish before but for a moment I thought maybe there was something in this, what the hell, there was no one around - no crowds and no Mobsters eyes to see what I was doing - and so I selfishly followed the prayer my sister spoke:

> *"God, I repent of my sinful ways and I ask for your forgiveness for denying you and for hurting others and myself. I believe you sent your son Jesus Christ to die on the cross to take the rap for my sins. I believe he was resurrected from death that I may have life. I receive Jesus into my heart today and I ask your Holy Spirit to come and teach me your ways."*

Whether I truly understood what I was saying I didn't really care, but after expressing the words 'Jesus come into my heart' something instantly changed. It felt like a ton of bricks had been lifted off my shoulders. I began to laugh uncontrollably and I knew at that moment something amazing had occurred - it was like mainlining and being on an instant high. Something had entered every part of my body, I felt clean, and I knew the God of my sister was real at that moment. For the first time ever I ran around the block as fast as I could in a state of freedom and release I'd never felt before. Fear and darkness fell away from my eyes and I could see colour with a vividness I had never experienced.

My sister took me for a drive around the city and it was like I saw blue sky for the first time in years. The sound of birdsong sent chills down my spine. 'Why hadn't I ever heard these birds before?' I asked myself. It seemed like my eyes had been opened like never before. I could see and recognise the beauty in everything and it sat in vivid contrast to my usual vision that scanned only muted grey and dark hues.

I felt so unworthy - my crimes and sins clanking behind like the chains they were - and I wondered why (or even how) this God would take the time to save me of all people. I also identified directly with the story my sister would 'bleat' on about - this Jesus - as someone who was hung out to dry and took the rap for something he was innocent of. That was like my life. Jesus took the rap for the sins of all man but in my case I felt I could never pay for my sins in several lifetimes. Jesus' blood paid for that and no mortal man's blood could pay for my actions. I understood the power of blood - I'd soaked in the blood of my enemies many times - but this was different. Even though I now saw with new eyes, my mind still doubted this experience was real.

My anxiety was that this God I couldn't see or touch would not truly set me free. Pressingly, I still had six hours to wait for my results and over those hours I prayed more than I had ever done in my life. I wanted this God to prove to me he was real by keeping me from death by Aids.

When I finally received the results of the blood test they were negative. I was ecstatic; I was not going to die of Aids. I believe it is no coincidence that sexual abuse led me to a gang life as much as it led me to God. Life throws up some strange curved balls. Whether I had Aids or not was not the point; a simple advertisement about the possibility of Aids led me to an answer when I hadn't even posed the question. It was like a strange intervention that seemed, at the time, to have no context.

Shockingly, I realised my conscience had lay dormant nearly all my life. Now that it was finally activated, I saw every detail of my life pass before my eyes like a drowning man. I realised that the consequences of my actions should've seen me rot in a lonely grave somewhere on the wrong side of the road. My lifestyle had made me a prime candidate to contract Aids, but I believe the God of my sister and the God of the Bible had kept me free from death for a purpose.

I finally saw that all my brothers in the gang had died for nothing, for a false belief. I found myself yelling out in a loud voice: 'Today I say I am worth far more than dying for a beer, a rumble, jail or a gang.' A new lease of life tore through every sinew in my body now that I knew the spirit of Jesus was real. That November day in 1989 changed my life sending me on a journey both harder than anything I had ever previously experienced, but more real than anything my past life could ever offer.

My new-found faith allowed me to know there was a God who was a higher authority than the Mob presidents, the police, the law, science or politics. I'd finally found a higher authority I could submit to. Submission was the flip side of life in the Mob. I had attained and fallen from the highest levels as a president so I understood what having power meant. Or so I thought. Power in the Mob was considered by the dogs to be the most privileged position on earth and no other authority mattered. Having served under past presidents, reaching the top level, laying down my patch and falling from grace, I had wandered in the valley of the lost with no one to arbitrate. In the end I couldn't live in this valley of darkness anymore; the only authority I had previously respected and trusted was my own savvy and streetwise nature and now it was an abandoned city. I realised that another president - a captain, a king, a God, a redeemer, call it what you like - existed above all other authority in the universe and was the catalyst that allowed me to abandon my own puny power base and to submit, trust and serve.

The words of the Bible consumed my every moment. Because I recognised God as a reality all biblical scripture took on new meaning. In the Mob, the president's words were regarded as ultimate truth. If you didn't act on these words then you were a fake, you weren't true red. This was all I knew. In some ways, such was the power of my revelation, it was an easy transition from the submission of dog leadership to the autonomy of God leadership.

I sealed my commitment to God with baptism. Originally I was born and baptised into a silent life of sexual abuse, while in the gang I was re-baptised into the firmament of violence, drugs, sexual excess and lawlessness. Now my life was to go through another baptism - I became a born again believer in Jesus Christ on March 1990 at the Te Atatu North Baptist Church amidst song, inspirational words and total immersion.

When I came out of the water I had the feeling that not only had I been let off my old life but that the chains had been unshackled from my neck and legs. For the first time in my life I felt truly free - free to be me.

As easy as it sounds from the outside, walking with God is no easy road. I had to examine the psychosis that was my life in detail, dismantle it piece by piece and put it back together again.

I had a battle to fight with every part of my mind, body and soul. The spirit may have entered my body but my very innards, my mind, my soul and my mouth were still fully Mongrel. I was a shambling contradiction, a walking-talking internal battlefield where forces from my past culture were fighting against the spirit of God for my life and allegiance. It was going to take time for things to reach a final alignment, it was either back to the dog or move towards a life with God. It was all about choice to stay with what I knew or to do a complete 180 degree u-turn. Maintaining my words of allegiance to this invisible God in my everyday life was to prove perhaps the hardest and most excruciating journey of my life.

True Red

Chapter Ten
RETURN TO THE DOG'S VOMIT

Taking a biblical view of life is a change of perspective not only in spirit but also in action. I was consumed by the content of the scriptures, especially reading about the biblical notions of repentance, confession and forgiveness. Repentance - changing one's mind or turning around 180 degrees - is an inward decision as well an outward momentum that moves you in a completely new direction in life. Central to repentance is confession - the outward expression of admitting your own failures and sins before God and those close to you. Forgiveness is an act of release from the bondage of anger, bitterness, resentment and revenge. It does not mean people are 'not guilty' but true forgiveness lifts the guilt of your abusers off your shoulders, giving it to God to deal with. Because God had forgiven me for my sins, I had to forgive others who had sinned against me. Not only this, but I had to grasp the nettle and seek the forgiveness of those I had wronged and take responsibility by confessing my own actions. Understanding these concepts I realised I had to be accountable, my first priority was to my own family now.

My son was two years old and I wanted to create a stable family vision for my wife and child. I started this process by telling my wife the truth of my life. I was compelled to confess, repent and ask my wife's forgiveness for my low life treatment of her over the years. I also wanted to confess to my wife the truth of my sexual life, something that could've placed her and the baby at risk. Urgency had seized me in its vice and I felt a compulsion to return home and get the truth out - I was like a ticking time bomb about to explode. I stood poised at the door of our house for a moment and thought about it. I was about to do something no Mongel Mob member in his right mind would even care two hoots about. I pondered the lifestyle I had led and the way I had treated my wife and all the women I had been with. It felt like a sawn-off shotgun poised at my head.

Family life had meant nothing to me, the patch ruled. The family was always last. My view of family was pretty much propelled by the Mob ethic regarding the treatment of women. I met my wife of the time as a young eighteen-year-old woman who knew nothing of gang life. She just happened to live next door to me at the time. After seducing her into my world she was quickly introduced to gang life, guns and violence. I was to become her lover, her father figure, her friend, her abuser, and her tormentor. I was her life without any path of escape now whether she liked it or not.

Living with me meant having weapons in the house constantly. She learned to clean and load my guns; we even slept with guns for protection. We had weapons in holes in the wall, holes in the floor, under the carpet, inside guitars, anywhere we could get good access to them. My wife never previously knew this lifestyle even existed in New Zealand. There were times the house would be shot up, so we had milk bottles lining the front lawn to hear enemies approach. We had a prospect sitting in our bedroom during the night to switch the light on if anything erupted. Nothing was ever private.

Women were never allowed to be involved in crimes and hits we had organised. We couldn't afford to take them with us for no other reason than if they were caught by the police and interrogated, the women were far more susceptible to being broken and speaking out. In the Mob you had to prove your faithfulness through your silence. Hear no evil, see no evil, speak no evil. To nark was to dig your own grave. The women in the gang were helpless and powerless to change anything including the violence. So much blood was spilt in our time. The oozing smell of blood not only stunk it was putrid. We lived on that, our women powerless to stop any of it. You couldn't take anyone to the hospital, as the police would then have to be involved. So people either died or were patched up pretty rough. My wife had to live with those realities - they quickly became her realities too.

Being beaten regularly was part and parcel of living with me. My rage was like a dog with lockjaw. While I had other women all over me as president, my wife had to sit and watch. She couldn't say a word without getting the bash. She was just my handbag who dressed the way I wanted, who cooked my eggs and satisfied my needs. My jealousy and covetousness was extreme. One wrong look would set me off in a rage. There was no women's argument I would ever listen to; they had no rights to speak. I loved my patch more than my woman.

The men dictated all the rules in the gang; there was no escaping that. Entering the gang women lost their innocence, their soul, their life, their friends, their past, their fun, their identity and their dignity. They were our punching bags, there to be a block shared by all. Even though I had claimed my wife as mine the urge to share her with the others was strong. It was dangerous for our partners to be alone without our protection especially when we were doing time in jail. Looking back now I realise they had to have their wits about them, otherwise they and their children were open slather for other Mobsters. I was very jealous of what was mine and if anyone tried to take what I owned they were going to pay.

If a woman left her man, the consequences were dire. They had no rights whatsoever. There were times my wife tried to run away simply to save her own life, but I hunted her down, threatening family and friends with their lives if they sheltered her. There was nowhere for her to run. I knew everyone she knew and in the state I was in, fear was always around the corner for her. I chased her like a rat, no one would dare put her up or if they did they'd have to deal with my wrath. Usually I would have let a woman run away as there were plenty more fish in the sea. For me to act so radically and violently, she must have really meant something to me.

We indoctrinated the young women into the way of the dog. They too learned Mob life was normal, that this life was all there was. This was pure love, the bash was love, abuse was love and this was true happiness. The Mob was love, the dog was love, and the Mongrel Mob was joy. Love was the big family of the Mob, a big patched-up family. You were meant to be a Mobster; you were born to be a Mobster.

Our families were born and bred in the Mob. Looking back now I see it was almost impossible for partners to rear the children any differently, there was no way to change their circumstances. There was no real choice for the women and children in our families.

The full feature film movie of my life and my treatment of women played out through my mind like a prolonged electric shock. I was completely devastated by my behaviour. I needed a whole new identity in the whanau and that meant trying to make some kind of amends for my atrocious treatment. It was a brutal legacy that I knew I could never really fully pay back in a lifetime.

I entered the doorway to our home, sat down and asked my wife's forgiveness for my past behaviour. Her reaction was understandable - she thought I was on drugs or something - and she had no sympathy. Was this for real or a joke? She tormented me for becoming a so-called Christian because she didn't really believe me. How could I come out with all this after all I'd put her and everyone else through? If I was for real I had to leave the Mob entirely. After all, I was still in the Mob; I looked like a Mobster and still acted like one. To her mind, I may have given my heart to the Lord but I was still in the Mob, dealing, fighting, and abusing. She hurled the line at me that 'your son will hate you'. I had failed to take on my full and proper responsibilities as a father. She believed nothing had changed in me by finding God. As far as she and many others were concerned I was a duplicitous fraud, trying to do right by covering up my true nature, endeavouring to save myself to get out of trouble. She knew I had chosen this new path, but she felt I had rushed into it boots and all and without thinking. It was all too fast.

I understood her pain and I didn't blame her. In many ways she was right: How could I be true to this new life while still attached like a limpet to the past in so many ways? I wasn't going to change overnight; it was going be a process. But my problem was that I didn't know how to exit the Mob except by death. I tried to prove that I could change through my own strength and that was the beginning of real problems.

For six months I committed myself to being a stay-at-home father. Attending church, something that was so foreign to me, allowed me to see families where husbands and wives and their kids were a family unit. It was a sight I had forgotten and did not have any understanding of. Like trying to envisage creatures from another galaxy I stared and tried to comprehend the concept of a normal family: 'Oh, is that what a family looks like?' I tried to emulate this new dynamic I'd seen but I was like a lost child in a hall of mirrors. I was to learn that past actions disappear slowly, old habits die hard. Things were changing for the better but a family visit to the beach still meant stopping at the pub across the road from the beach, the family having to settle for peering out of the car window at the sand and waves while I walked inside for an ale or twenty.

While I tried hard to live out a biblical based life, desperately wanting to be good, it seemed my past was always lingering in my soul ready to emerge again. It's funny how one simple act can drastically change your life's direction leaving in its trail rash decisions, devastation and regret. In May 1990 we had just finished building our second home. Celebrating this milestone, I picked up a beer and drank it. Drinking more, I opened myself up to my old life again and in that single moment of sipping a beer I drank in all the ghosts of my past. All my addictions and demons instantly kicked in, the ugly side of me resurrected itself and all hell broke loose. I abused the neighbours and tormented and physically assaulted my wife in a drunken stupor that was a reprise of all my worst gang behaviour. In the space of half a day I had reverted back to my old self, silent, explosive and full of rage. Old dog voices started to intrude on my mind: 'What the hell am I doing? Who in their right mind as a Mobster finds God, has a wife, a child, two houses and a good life? No one. Why should I be any different? I don't deserve them. This is not being true red.' I believed these words, I swallowed them deep and allowed them to control my emotions, speech, and actions.

Lacking resolution, my wife and I separated and our two homes were sold. I felt God had abandoned me and everything was lost. Self-pity and the cold hand of failure overtook me. I had to find a way to survive and rebuild my life again.

Mob business became the centre of my life again. Skunner, another brother from the Waikato, shifted to Auckland and aligned himself with me in my desperate state. We had similar views on a new vision for the Mob's future and when we realised this we developed a tight new relationship. Three of us climbed One Tree Hill and spoke and prayed to the great bulldog in the sky to bless us and dedicate us to a new era. Our prayer to the bulldog in the sky was made up of mongrel talk and reciprocal dog barking. We decided to adopt the sentiments of another newly formed chapter 'Mongrel Mob New Zealand' which had been instigated by brothers from inside Paremoremo Prison. The guys joining this chapter were made up of those who'd moved away from their own chapters for various reasons. Additionally, the prison boys wanted a new chapter for those who had been released but who'd lost faith in the chapters on the outside they'd traditionally been associated with. Aligning with Mongrel Mob New Zealand allowed us to still be pure mongrel and continue the 'red' ethic, but in a modified form. All the old guard of presidents were dead, and this chapter was to be run leaderless. I became a freelance Mongrel Mob member who was accessible to all other chapters and to lone brothers who wanted to change direction. We wanted to be Mobsters at the same time as being part of mainstream society, a balance that to an outsider looked problematic. I was patched now under Mongrel Mob New Zealand but quickly I found it didn't satisfy my quest for a way ahead for the Mob - it didn't fulfill me any more. Nothing seemed to work, it was either change or continue on as I had planned.

I became a drifter. In a state of despair, I returned again to my regular haunts to wallow in the old Mob atmosphere. What else was I to do, where else was I to go? Separating from my wife and baby messed with my head big time. I returned to the old haven in Taumarunui where I'd originally found comradeship and brotherhood with the King Country Mongrel Mob. The guys were surprised when I arrived on their doorstep - they knew where I was at - and I was grateful they received me with open arms. Your walk is always remembered in the Mob; once a brother always a brother. They patched me up again. But to tell you the truth I never wore it on my back again and instead I kept it in my bag. With a twinge in my heart I knew the patch didn't really mean anything to me anymore. It was then that I knew something had changed in me. Very quickly I saw things weren't the same; rising through the ranks, becoming a president and a charismatic leader and then reverting to a lowly de-patched member was a real statement about loss of power and mana. I knew it and so did the boys. Maybe they had patched me up again as an act of brotherly sympathy.

I thought I'd find comfort in being a re-patched member of the home gang again and returning to the vomit of the dog. But the vomit did not have its intoxicating flavour and allure anymore; it was now bitter, dark and lifeless. I couldn't even stick to the rules of the pad; I didn't even respect the leadership. So I basically did my own thing. Back in the black and red environment I was both uncontrollable and almost crazy - I was back in dog mode but only obliquely. The old pain of losing my presidency felt like it was constantly pounding in my head with a rhythm for revenge. In retaliation I smashed up the whole pad. I wanted my presidency back and that meant taking out the current leader. Frenzied though I was I had enough savvy to realise I couldn't take on the whole Mob at once and I had to let it go.

I tried to find solace and peace in my old friend - sex with easy women who hung out in the gang scene. Again I found myself with a new partner but our relationship was marred by my abusive and violent nature. Amazingly, she had some knowledge of Christ and often spoke of how the both of us needed this spirit to heal our wounds. However, at the time I wasn't listening. As far as I was concerned God was dead.

My uncontrollable temper and vicious fists meant I was summoned to court again for assault charges, this time against my new partner. I did four months periodic detention for this assault but the sentence was never going to change my behaviour. Without any remorse I bashed her again and I was charged with assault. But this time it was a lot more serious. I now had the possibility of a ten-year sentence. Tired of being in this continual cycle of violence I tried to find an escape. Waiting for the hearing to come before the court, I went on a new search for identity. I turned to my Maori roots.

Lost in my own mind I tried to discover who I really was within my own culture realising I needed a new identity apart from the Mob. Really, there was no turning back. In the Mongrel Mob our Maori identity meant nothing to us, but I turned towards that side of me now for some sort of sustenance. I thought about wearing a facial tattoo or having the moko, as somehow this would prove my Maori identity and stop my slide into an abyss. The people I began to hang out with influenced me, instilling in me how my Maoriness, reo and tikanga would give me new life and a real identity. I began to learn Maori and then committed myself to having my face tattooed with the lines of my life, just as the old ancestors had done in previous generations. Many of the guys in the gang had their faces tattooed but for very different reasons than the traditional. My body was completely tattooed with the road signs of my Mongrel Mob life - every emblem of the dog was etched somewhere on my skin - but now my face would reveal a new transition in my life.

As the ta-moko artist began to draw the lines on my face I saw this as a transition into a new stage of life. Eventually the artist completed my moko over five separate sessions and a long period of time. I allowed him open slather with my face but I told him he was to leave the ihu or nose section for a pattern of my own design. I wanted the lines here to represent my dream to combine all the gangs as one, not by our own power but under the authority of God. This still remains a real dream of mine.

Later I found myself at a gathering of Maori staying at Nukutapu Marae in Taupo, some of whom had supported my trust in Auckland. But the words spoken at the hui failed to touch me, they made little sense and, reflecting on it now, I realise I was too bonded to mongrelism to truly see the environment around me. I love being Maori - speaking the reo, knowing my history - and this meant my heart was always asking questions about where true life existed. In retrospect, having a moko never really changed anything in me, it didn't change my dark heart and soul, and it only gave me the outward image of being Maori. After a period of time the search for a true identity in my Maoriness never satisfied my soul's craving for truth and the meaning of my life; it never brought peace to my heart; it didn't heal my marriage; it didn't give me hope or a purpose to live my life out meaningfully; it didn't change anything in my life. I felt there had to be something better than this particular life I was living.

While having a shower at Nukutapu the room suddenly changed before me. I found myself in a vision of prison bars and a long tunnel with white light at the end of it. Then a loud voice spoke to me: 'You'll never get clean like that my son, only my love and my word will clean you, direct you and save you. Return to me or return to prison.' I knew it was God and I spoke out loud: 'Lord you know my situation. If you want me to serve you my life is in your hands.' God spoke again: 'I will send someone to pick you up, I have a plan and a purpose for your life.' At that point I knew where I should be and who my master really was and it wasn't the dog and it wasn't the moko. I walked out of that shower block to find a King Country Mob member had arrived at the marae to pick me up and return me to Taumarunui. I was momentarily stunned.

As we drove back to Taumarunui, the brother who escorted me told me he knew the Lord Jesus too. I was astounded. He told me how he did not know how to get out of the hole he was in. I told him I was going to find a way out; I was leaving. Now I knew with a certainty that God really was on my case.

I walked into the Taumarunui Baptist Church and asked the local pastor to pray for me. Not only did he do this but he was a great help to me in trying to sort out my domestics. He came around to see me and accompanied me to court to face the assault charges and we prayed for the Lord's will to be done. Whatever the accumulated debris in my life I was now ready to face up to anything, whether that meant freedom or another stint inside. For the first time in my life I could honestly accept with equanimity whatever judgement was delivered. I also knew that God would never leave me or forsake me and it was up to me now to show some commitment no matter what happened legally.

I eventually appeared in court for assault with all the odds stacked against me. Miraculously, the charges were eventually dropped in August 1991: my partner had lost her memory as a witness in the dock and the prosecution couldn't mount a credible case without her oral testimony.

At that point I knew there was someone else looking out for my welfare. Convinced it was God, I totally rededicated my life to the Lord Jesus Christ. I enrolled in a Baptist rehabilitation programme at a halfway house in Rotorua. Over a four-month period I witnessed how these good people put up with my antics in a bid to see the light of day.

While I was here a Maori-based Bible school came to my attention. I wanted to learn more of what the Bible taught about life. This was the beginning of the process of readjusting my 'dog' psyche to a 'God' mindset. This would mean dismantling everything I had ever known or been taught about life, love, hate, violence, relationships, leadership, obedience, authority, spirituality, whanau, loyalty, respect, humility, good, evil and the existence of God. I realised God had allowed me to return to my own vomit and put it under a microscope to vividly magnify the stark realities of my old life. I was able to see with new eyes, to smell and touch the truth of what it was I had been wallowing in for most of my life. In my old state I couldn't see the hatred, the violence, the revenge and the lawlessness that was my life and normal world view.

One scripture that spoke to me was Psalm 17:4:

' *... by the word of your lips I have kept myself from the path of the destroyer.* '

In the Mob I didn't know God, I didn't know his word, and without it I had allowed the destroyer (death or violence) to enter my life. Everything around me smelt of death and its pungent aroma permeated all the brother's lives. But as clear as it must have been to outsiders, we couldn't see it or smell it in our midst. Until you step out of the boundaries you live within you do not really see the reality of your life and of those around you. This dark revelation - the septic pit I had lived in for years - made me realise this was not where I really wanted to be anymore. I wasn't born to be a Mobster and neither were my brothers. The Mob was a lie I had embraced.

I knew that God was asking me to abandon everything and to follow Jesus - to be a fisher of men not a killer of men. To accomplish this task I had to leave all of my old life behind - put to death my past, leave my old cemetery clothes in the pit of darkness and replace them with garments of salvation and praise. To do this I had to learn to be obedient and to come under a new authority, something I'd fought against for a major part of my life. I had been my own authority for years. The Bible says the fear of God is the beginning of wisdom. The word fear here actually means to be obedient. Coming before a big God means obedience, humility and submission so the wisdom of life may be imparted to you. Wisdom is hard to teach to a haughty or prideful person as they think they already know everything. That was me all over.

Everyday a new scripture would cause me to sit and ponder my future.

Proverbs 3: 5-6 says:

> *'Trust in the Lord with all your heart and lean not on your*
> *own understanding, in all your ways acknowledge him,*
> *and he will make your paths straight.'*

I trusted the Lord; he had released me from a situation that could have sent me on another spiral of negativity for years. I didn't want to lean on my old Mongrel Mob beliefs anymore; it was going to send me to jail or six feet under. I wanted to acknowledge Him so He could show me a new pathway for life and because He was now my captain I believed His word as plain spiritual truth. I knew I had been given a second chance to create new life, not to resurrect the mask of death.

Some may say: Why take the God way out to seek change? Isn't that a hypocritical cop out? Isn't it a bit extreme? Isn't it enough just being a good well-rounded responsible citizen who works hard, plays sport, takes responsibility for the kids and family, pays taxes, votes, supports friends in times of need, parties on, owns a home and a car, is educated, or works for the local marae? Well no it isn't, not for someone like me. I tried that life and I always fell back to my old ways and reverted to the dog. More importantly, those elements of life could never change my black heart that was so full of hatred and despair. Until this was wiped away life would be underpinned by my dark heart. Its raw and nescient emotions, deposited slime on everyone and everything it touched. I started to glimpse that only through the knowledge of and submission to the spirit of God through Jesus Christ could I deal with the deep issues in my heart. I realised the voices that fed my mind for years were real spiritual entities and it would take a belief in the spiritual realm to combat a spiritual problem. No mundane secular life where problems are treated with antidepressants or simply suppressed was going to do this for me. Those options don't get rid of the voices. Jesus said:

> *'...the good man brings good things out of the good stored in his heart while the evil man brings evil things from the evil stored in his heart.'* [7]

With my heart in such an evil and broken condition the only fruit that would ever ripen on my tree would be rotten. Not only that, but this rot would permeate and consume the lives of those around me. For that reason I decided to enroll in Te Whare Amorangi Bible School at Pukekohe where I could learn scriptural principles for life. I had been in many tight corners but this was to be the greatest struggle of my life and the most life changing and satisfying.

True Red

Chapter Eleven
RENEWING THE MIND

I was one of the first students to enter the Whare Amorangi Bible School at the Te Puna-o-te-ora complex at Pukekohe. It was a place where I was to learn the word of God and how to apply it to my everyday life. I also had to mix with people I didn't know and couldn't control. In other words, people who had never lived in a gang and probably had no idea about the shadowy world I came from. I arrived on the scene in my leather reggies and boots, my slurred speech, a full facial moko, long hair and an outlaw gang reputation - I was wild, raw and as rough as guts. I didn't enter into this world singing songs of praise to Zion that's for sure, but nevertheless I was open to learning something new. I must have seemed totally out of place, especially as the people here had never met anyone like me before. I believe many of them struggled with my look and my very being when I arrived.

Interestingly, Pukekohe was a Black Power stronghold. They were people who hated me for what I once stood for, especially after a series of confrontations that had just recently erupted between the blacks and the

Mongrels. And they knew who I was all right. As it happened, the Black Power pad was in close proximity to the bible school. The situation was almost laughable but it didn't dampen my resolve to continue my pursuit of God. In my mind I was already reconciled with Black Power. I had no beef with them. I had previously visited the Black Power pad in South Auckland to inform their leader I was finished with the gangs and that I was immigrating to God's gang. He accepted my decision and wished me well. It's funny how God sends you to places that tip you on your head, teach you tolerance or expose things in your life that you need to overcome. This was certainly one of those situations.

There was criticism of my decision to enter Bible school and in the state I was in - in terms of appearance alone - I wasn't easily accepted. There were those who thought I was there for the women or simply to steal the monetary tithes and offerings. There were others that didn't believe I had the stamina to last the distance. But they were simply judging a rough tattooed exterior that seemed to bark and growl in a slurred accent: a heavyweight gang member who couldn't be changed or trusted. The director of the course put me on a two-week trial period, after which they'd check my progress. Would I steal the tithes or kick holes in the walls or would I actually handle the pressure and be able to do the work?

It was inevitable I would come up against a brick wall of prejudice considering the perception of gangs amongst the general public was one of complete disdain. Coming out of the Mongrel Mob gang was a hard ask. Sometimes I felt suffocated by the public's labels - a leopard never changes its spots, once a gang member always a gang member - and those sentiments bound me to the curse of the 'dog'. How was I ever going to move myself out of deprivation and paint myself on to a new canvas?

I lived a life of extremes and it was going to take another 'extreme' to replace it. In my old life I would have openly vented my anger at the criticisms of people and taken out a nasty revenge. However, this time I had to overlook all that, I just clenched my fists silently and carried on. I was determined to prove I could last the distance and change.

I believed in Acts 17: 26 where it says:

> *'He [God] determined the times set for them, and the exact*
> *places where they should live ...'*

These words made a big impression on me and I knew this was where I was supposed to be; God had challenged me to do this and to stay here for a time. The law was out to get me, Mobsters and other gangs were on my case, all my old relationships had disintegrated, my old leaders had passed away - it was all lost and empty back there - and there was nowhere else to go. And when the pressure really came on, I knew I didn't want to die in failure in my old environment or in prison.

I may have felt I was a stranger in a strange land but I was now in a place where I would learn more about myself than I had anywhere else. In a sense it was a place that God had hidden me, teaching me stability, showing me the difference between right and wrong, giving me life boundaries and ensuring I respected and actually learned to love people. All this in a place that my former consciousness would have instinctively scanned as enemy territory and with a bunch of strangers whose beliefs meant nothing to me. It was totally contrary to what I had learned to be as a Mongrel Mob member.

Perhaps one of the biggest adjustments I had to learn in this environment was how to relate to people other than Mobsters. At least with the Mobsters

I knew how they thought, acted and spoke and I could take anything they could dish out - their actions and their hakihaki (life scabies) were in full view; their hatred of the world shouted uncompromisingly and nothing was hidden. But in this new environment I was living with new people, people from different nationalities and backgrounds. I couldn't understand their ways or their vocabulary and I found it difficult to read their body language or their minds. I had to learn to cook and clean, deal with new male and female relationships and converse and learn with all sorts of people. I lacked the same shape and form that had nurtured the people I was now with; I had little idea about how they viewed and related to the world. The fact that it was a Maori run organisation made this transition a little easier perhaps, but it was still very hard and frustrating. I felt like a total fish out of water.

I was like a newborn baby who had cast off its protective womb - which effectively is what the Mob was - and abandoned all my old rights and powers. Now I was in a place God had placed me to learn submission to his word and unconditional love. For all my Mob life submission did not exist, that was reserved for the president and the great bulldog in the sky above. All my Mob relationships had been based on some form of conditioned brutalisation.

I spent most of my days on the premises where our daily routine consisted of classes and prayer times. Off site I had to learn to live in a house with six others, to share the household workload - vacuuming, washing dishes, cooking dinner, laundry - and train myself to rise early to get to 8.30am classes. Time management and domestic chores were a foreign land to me. Usually I never rose till midday, I never had breakfast (beer was my daily food), I seldom washed, and for leisure I commonly watched mafia and porno films. I always wore red and black leathers covered with Mongrel Mob emblems and I was a ruru (night owl) used to partying and clubbing through all hours of the night. Housework, gathering and preparing food were never my jobs, they were the roles of my women or of the prospects assigned to me.

Even simple things like greeting someone became problematic. In the Mob we greeted each other by spitting on our hands and clenching our fists together, with a hearty 'Seig Heil doggy'. No-one ever greeted anyone with a kiss - that was so alien to me I viewed it as a sign of total weakness. To shake hands, kiss someone or hongi as a greeting may have been standard in my new world but it was totally foreign and abhorrent to me. Apart from anything, the way I looked usually scared people and often made them close up shop, lock up their tills or take a step backwards if approached. Nevertheless, I took to greeting people in the new manner, even if it felt alien to my body or people looked at me sideways. Mixing with women was fraught with problems for me. Greeting and kissing a woman in a cordial manner was a very new and weird experience. The new environment allowed women the same privileges as men and even more authority in some cases. I found that hard to fathom coming from a world where women had little or no rights at all. Interacting with women on this course, some who had authority over me or others who simply contributed to the class discussions, was challenging. But I put self-control into practice, something I had never previously had to do. Instead of thinking about sexually abusing or beating women I was now saying hello and kissing them on the cheek in a respectful and cordial manner. Who would have thought?

Much of the language used in the classes or in normal conversation was sometimes above my head and the way I talked always seemed harsh and in many cases incomprehensible to the teachers and students. Remnants of the dog language were still in my mouth like congealed vomit and some also thought the years of drugs had affected the way I marshaled my thoughts and delivered my words. Even in prayer meetings I was a distraction to people. I was used to speaking at volume to hundreds of gang members all at once, so I would pray at the top of my voice. When I was slain in the spirit and fell to the ground it engendered nervous unease because people thought I was either drunk or acting disrespectfully in the house of the Lord. They would try to kick me out and I seemed, what with one thing and another, to be always disturbing the peace. For instance, accidentally knocking the pool cue against the light shade caused anxiety, and people would think I was ready to erupt into violence. Sometimes it felt like I just couldn't win and I often queried whether I really fitted in. The only time I felt really comfortable was when I was having a big kai (feast). But little by little I learnt to be submissive to the teachings and the course leaders, as well as being sensitive to others around me.

I arrived at the bible school in my gang gears as they were all I had. I would wear black, long-sleeved shirts, a leather jacket and leather pants or reggies with heavy boots. But one thing I never did was reveal my tattoos except for the moko on my face. Once when I was asked to speak at another church, the only pants I had were my reggies with a gaping hole in the crotch. People were offended by my appearance as I delivered a sermon, but my fellow Bible classmates, used to me by now, stayed straight-faced. Because my body was completely covered in Mongrel Mob tattoos it was always a challenge as to what to wear. Even with my own kids I would seldom undress or go swimming with them in a public place lest I cause a confrontation and get stepped-out by an enemy who'd taken offence at my tattoos. At a Christian camp I attended I was told to cover up because the women felt it was inappropriate for their children to see my fully tattooed body. In the heat of summer I covered my body in sweltering black clothes to lessen any offence. Sometimes I felt like turning back to the mongrel dog because people here just didn't want to accept me. It was at times like this that I felt extremely lonely but I had nowhere to go, nowhere to call home except the one I was currently living in. However, I fought these thoughts and covered up my body, staying with a humble demeanor for God's sake. It took me a long time to replace my reggies and gang regalia with plain clothes, but I have never replaced my tattoos or moko - they remind me of where I came from.

I remember discussions about my image in the community. The first thing people should see in us is our Christ-like nature not our cultural or ethnic outlook. That was pretty hard to achieve while wearing a moko as it provoked not only strange reactions but also judgement. On Bible school trips around New Zealand my presence was considered intimidating and shops and petrol stations locked up their doors, drawers and cupboards when I turned up with a bunch of Bible-bashing Christians. As far as I am concerned this stereotyping is other people's problem, not mine.

I sat in a classroom for two years with many different guest lecturers teaching about the books of the Bible. Being taught in this manner - sitting under a person of authority was unfamiliar territory for me. In addition to this, I had no real knowledge about the Bible but I was hungry for more understanding of the word. A good level of literacy was almost unknown in the Mob and no-one ever read anything except comics and magazines with pictures; most of the guys were semi-literate and everything was verbal. The exceptions were our treasurers who had to be literate to be able to tell us how much money we had in the bank. Despite this semi-literate environment and my immersion in it, reading the word became a passion and I had so much zeal for reading and studying the Bible that it became the only thing I could hold on to that was real, that would calm me and control my actions.

Living in Black Power territory and having those guys as neighbours was like having a permanent thorn in my side. They knew who I was, they hated me, and everything I stood for as a Mobster and also as a Bible-basher. Jesus's greatest commandment to his followers was to love your neighbour, something I was determined to live out with these guys. If I believed in this teaching then I had to live it out in action. One night the Black Power neighbours had a loud party that really irked me. Later that night when someone threw a beer bottle at my door my first reaction was to jump over the fence and smash someone with a baseball bat. However, God spoke to me to leave the bat and not to act in my old reactive way. It was hard enough walking past the Black Power houses everyday on my way to Bible study. The provocation got on my wick, but I simply had to let it go and ignore them. Another day I heard my family's house had been robbed by the Black Power, and as a new believer in God I had to deal with this outside my old mindset. In the book of Matthew Jesus said:

> 'You have heard it said, "Love your neighbour and hate your enemy." But I tell you: Love your enemy and pray for those who persecute you that you may be sons of your father in Heaven.'[8]

Being a 'son of God' and a follower of Jesus in action means loving your neighbours and your enemies. When the voices from my past screamed for retribution, I had to fight the old ways, humble myself before God and pray for the Black Power brothers who'd trespassed my family's home. Who would have ever thought a Mobster would ever consider blessing an enemy? That could only truly be an act of God because it certainly ran contrary to all my old instincts. In the end I confronted the Black Power president in Papakura face to face. As I've said, usually I would have smashed someone to get my family's belongings back, however, this time I opted for another way to deal with it. I humbly sought the leader's grace to investigate the allegation that some of his boys had not only trespassed but also stolen some of my family's household goods. Within half an hour a black car turned up at the whanau's house and all the stolen goods were returned. This 'love your enemy' stuff had legs.

I remember once turning up to my Black Power neighbour's home with bread to preach the Gospel. While I sat and talked to them about Jesus they reciprocated with accounts of past Mongrel Mob ventures against their gang. While food was prepared for me their cheeky kids poked their defiant tongues out at me. But I must say that after fifteen years in Pukekohe they have come to see me for who I am and they have slowly started to accept me, although I know they think I have the most boring life. Hei aha!

Daily anger was an emotion I had to contend with but the real problem was that I never really acknowledged where this anger resided. I had been invited by an Indian minister to attend a function in Fiji. I had no access to banks or post offices at that point and I kept what precious items I had on me at all times, including the earnings I'd set aside for this trip. At the time I was still training at the gym to keep my body in shape and I left my money belt behind the gym's counter. After my workout I returned to find the money had been stolen. I did my block, my anger rose up and I came close to attacking someone. My mentors were so calm about it I couldn't comprehend why they did nothing. Maybe it was because they knew God was trying to show me something I couldn't see, and that small situations sometimes expose something in you that needs attention. I realised right there and then that my anger controlled me like a vicious dictator and I had to admit it. I was seized by this strong conviction and the pastors encouraged me to ask forgiveness of the thieves, retreat from my attitude and apologise to the guys I yelled at. If God intended me to attend the function in Fiji He would provide for it if my attitude was right. As is often the way when we embrace the teachings of Jesus, money arrived by donation and allowed me to travel to Fiji.

I vividly remember one particular spoken message changing my life as I mentally wrestled with those I thought were against me. During a session we called devotions a student was asked to share a word from scripture with the class and his story of Moses crossing the Red Sea had a real impact on me. The student spoke of God creating a way for Moses and his people to cross the Red Sea that they, in their humanness, were unable to achieve. The seas opened up allowing the people to cross. Their Egyptian enemies pursued them but were eventually destroyed by God who allowed the seas to swallow them up. This story became relevant to my life as God had allowed my enemies to be buried in the abyss and I realised I had no need to seek utu for anything anymore. Psalm 143:11-12 speaks of a God who will:

'...preserve my life; in his righteousness, bring me out of trouble. Silence my enemies; destroy all my foes for I am your servant..'

Understanding this I knew God would deal with things if I just served Him - I made a commitment to be a servant - my need for utu and revenge died in me that day, I didn't have to rely on that as an answer to a problem. This was a huge release for me coming, as I did, from a background where most of the brothers I loved and lived with died violent and lonely deaths nurtured in a world of revenge. But here I am, still alive and well, and the only reason is my belief in a God who is my refuge and who I serve.

Part and parcel of Bible school curriculum was attending church services. Going to church was probably the most alien thing I have ever had to face, contrasting so vividly, as it does, with gang pad life. Here people pray, raise their hands in worship, clap to happy Jesus songs, listen to Bible messages, drink communion wine and hand their money over in a velvet bag. Sometimes every kind of anti-church, anti-missionary and anti-Pakeha sentiment came to mind as I sat in the pew. While I believed in the word my mind was often still in gang mode, suspicious of people not my own. Voices in my head often spoke against the congregation who had their hands lifted to God. 'What kind of weakness is it to raise your hands to God?' the voices would query. I remained paranoid that everyone was criticising and judging me for being a Maori and a gang member. 'Those people don't know me or what I've been through, they were never in the gang.' These thoughts had the potential to become as destructive as a virulent cancer in my journey back to God and I knew my old thinking had to die or I would never be able to accept people for what they are. It was simple. If I wanted people to accept me for what

I was I had to learn to accept others as they are, and none more so than my brothers and sisters who attended church. I had to silence the spirit of indifference, antipathy and division in me. There are still things about the way church is conducted that irk me but I have to simply keep my mind on God and what he is trying to teach me. I often wonder how different church would be if there were hundreds of gang members in the congregation - I dream of that day.

Having powerful Maori men as teachers and mentors was probably my saving grace. They were committed to me for the long haul, building a trust and a level of relationship that allowed me to openly speak to them in a safe environment about anything. There was never any personal criticism but nor were they frightened to correct me when I was acting inappropriately. There was always strong and wise counsel available to address my personal baggage and all the stuff I didn't understand. And it was advice about the simple things of life that was particularly handy. For instance, I had huge problems with Inland Revenue but with solid guidance I was able to settle my affairs in an orderly fashion. They stood by me when I fell or hit a brick wall, but they always left the final decision to me. Without strong men around who had no fear about confronting me I would never have survived this particular journey.

On one occasion the course leaders performed an act so foreign I had no reference point or understanding that steadied me. Our class was asked if we would allow the course leaders to wash our feet. I was dumbstruck at this request. Why would those above me ever think of belittling themselves by stooping down to such a lowly act? Little did I realise that Jesus the Messiah had washed the feet of his servants to teach them that leadership is not about control and force but about servant-hood.

Just as Jesus served men so we should not feel humiliated serving others. My view of leadership was always about fronting up, being staunch and stern and ruling with an iron fist. To wash the feet of plebeian low-lifers - those of the underclass or prospects - was ludicrous in my eyes. Even for a Maori male to submit to the shame of having his feet washed by a leader or washing the feet of someone else verged on total humiliation and shame. As the leaders bent down with water and oil and washed our feet it broke the pride in me with the force of a jailbird breaking rocks; there was nothing so lowly the leaders would not do to serve me and to illustrate their love for me and their obedience to Christ. No one had ever served me in this manner and I was overwhelmed with tears - it was another turning point for me. This action became an example for the way I was to treat others.

It would be wrong to assume that confronting these issues always changed me on the spot; sometimes it was a process that took years to accomplish and there are still many challenges I face daily. This has meant holding on to God's precepts in the word, letting it percolate into my mind and body, having self-control to enact that word and then battling the old demonic voices that controlled my mind and body. These demonic voices are entities that scream out like heroin dependent cells for the things that have fed them in the past. I'd allowed these deceiving voices to control every part of my life like an addict and opened myself up to actions totally contrary to the word of God. The outcome was a litany of crimes that threw-up violence, rape, hatred, murder and malice. When these demonic voices spoke to me my will and mind agreed with them and acted in a manner that seemed satisfying and good at the time. Evil, in my Mongrel mind, was good. Whatever the bulldog voice spoke I believed.

To combat this I tried to realign my inner and outer self to God's will and his word. The old thoughts we pay homage to in our minds can keep us bonded to the past but if we allow the 'renewing of the mind', as scripture puts it, change can occur. For me this involved a super-human effort of self-control. Because my life had been so full of bad behaviour it had to be rooted out over a long period before I could trust myself to live back in society.

My security now lay in the word of God; I believed passionately, and slowly but surely it began to anchor my mind and actions. What previously would have enraged me and sent me down a path of utu became tamed, and eventually my reactions and emotions changed to being in harmony with the mind of God, to tolerate, to love and serve people.

With this new shift in focus I took on a new name. Many characters in the Bible were given new names when their lives changed: Abram became Abraham, Jacob became Israel, Saul became Paul. Jesus gave Simon Bar-Jonah (Simon son of Jonah) the new name Cephas (Aramaic for 'rock') otherwise known as Peter, so that he would know who he should be in the future.[9] This was also an old Maori custom, to change or add an additional name to signify a major event in life. I began to use my middle name, Tuhoe, an ancestral name I was told signified bravery. I was born Patrick, named Bo by my immediate whanau, identified as Tara Rangi in Australia, nicknamed Bruno in the Mongrel Mob and rebirthed into Christianity as Tuhoe Isaac.

Chapter Twelve
CONQUERING GIANTS

Confronting new relationalship issues was only part of the process of my transformation. The more pressing matter for me was learning how to apply the word of God to my daily life. Perhaps the one single subject of the Bible I really had to grapple with was the biblical notion of sin, and the power and impact it had on my life. Being steeped in Mongrel values like hatred, rape, fear and intimidation, misogyny, theft, revenge and violence - I believed these foundation stones of the Mob were all there was to life. All these entrenched Mongrel thought patterns and prejudices I cherished and served were embedded in my psyche like a rusty fishhook. They were like parasites infesting my very soul. Let's face it, there's only so much destructive lifestyle you can pursue before it all catches up with you. I had to ask myself, did I want to keep living by these principles or not? I didn't and my old thinking had to be extracted like an abscessed tooth, the giants of my past had to be conquered if I was to survive and embrace real meaning in life. Beginning a new life took a lot of soul-searching, it wasn't simple and it didn't happen overnight.

At one time I tried to change these features of my life by simply trying to be good, following people I believed supported me, and creating a positive environment. I quickly grew frustrated, I could never accomplish much no matter how I tried, I always seemed to revert back to the way of the Mongrel - I couldn't control it. I had no understanding what I was actually dealing with until I became aware of the power of sin. Eager to learn I listened intently how sin, which literally means 'missing the mark', was a spirit that entered the world as a consequence of the disobedient actions of one man and now works in the mind and soul of all men.[10] It has its own law scripture calls the law of the sinful nature. That nature caused me to be hostile and disobedient to God's ways, to always commit evil even if I desired to do good. The sinful nature can never do good.[11] Because I had no conscience or recognition of the existence of sin or the law of sinful nature in me it wouldn't have mattered how hard I tried to change my environment, my look, my ways or even my daily routine, mongrelism would always prevail.

Sexual immorality, impurity, debauchery, idolatry and witchcraft, hatred, discord, jealousy, rage, selfish ambition, dissensions, factions, envy, drunkenness, orgies and the like, are aspects of the sinful nature mentioned in the scriptures.[12] Throughout my life I had 'missed the mark'. Sinful desire was what I dished out to people every day; I immersed myself in it every day; I unleashed it every day; I lived with it every day. I was it every day.

Little did I know, these activities allowed demonic spirits a right to infect my attitudes and thoughts and influence my actions - in reflection I saw demonic activity surround me constantly. However, more devastating to me was the idea that those who live like this will not inherit the Kingdom of God. This is reiterated in the following:

'The man who sows to please his sinful nature, from that nature will reap destruction; the one who sows to please the Spirit will reap eternal life'.[13]

Few understood the seductive forces of destruction like I did and I had to erect NO EXIT signs to stop continuing down that path anymore. I didn't want to continue with it. I wanted to please the spirit and dwell in the eternal kingdom of God - a place I know I have access to right now, not simply after my death.

In the past I wanted to live a 'good life' that included both a gang mentality and the tenants of mainstream society. Sitting in this place I quickly came to realise without the knowledge of God and submission to the spirit of Christ I could never accomplish this. I tripped up every time and I continually returned to the old mentality because my mind was still totally obedient to the law of the sinful nature, to the law of the dog. I was a slave to sin, a slave to the dog - it ruled me. By buying into that nature I was unruly, uncontrollable, unteachable, I would always be a hardcore Mobster. My sin had allowed demonic spirits to dwell in my thoughts and sublimely speak to me, influencing my every decision and action. I realised I had lived a life contrary to the ways of God.

I finally saw my entire life laid bare before God, the hidden deeds of my life now exposed to the light, I just had to admit this was truly who I was. Guilt ridden, and astonished how vulnerable knowing that stuff made me feel, I spent hours contemplating in my room alone, hiding my secret deeds and inner self from the world. I had to stare at the developing darkroom photo, slowly emerging in to focus, and accept it for what it was. I knew I had to do something about this but I wasn't ready to acknowledge my sin straight away. It took me months to admit them to myself, to God and to my peers.

Many months into the Bible course I remember being woken up late one night by the voice of the Holy Spirit of God who told me to get out of bed and write down all of my sins. I didn't know why or for what purpose, I was just obedient to the gentle voice that spoke to me that night. I sat up and began to write. Hundreds of scenarios flashed through my mind, my memory became flooded with the recollection of past events, things I had openly committed as well as shameful acts I had carried out in secret. It was almost unbearable to remember.

At this stage I wanted to admit to myself and to God who I was, I wanted my sin gone, dusted off and dealt with. I was ready to acknowledge those things to the world. I knew Jesus's blood paid the price for my life and now was the time I really had to surrender everything to him. I began to write every memory that came to mind on the page and I could have written a number of books that night. The more I wrote the more I remembered and the more eye-opening and soul searching the exercise became. Listing the heinous crimes of my life enabled me to see the full extent of the crooked pathway I'd walked and it reminded me of walking without a torch down a very dark path overgrown with gorse. I saw the full extent of the consequences of my actions. God exposed a light on every aspect of my life.

This experience took me back to my childhood. I couldn't blame my parents for the way I turned out, they gave me everything within their means to give me a life and I am grateful to them. I thought perhaps my warped view of life was a result of my sexual abusers? In many ways I could say this was partly true, they had created emotional wounds in me that I hid from everyone because of shame. However, my response to their actions caused me to emulate their very actions, I too was to become a sexual predator. I didn't want to burden my family with my problems so I left home to find my own way, to seek my own answers to life. Soon I began to search out companionship through sexual relationships, which became manic in the years to come. Sexual depravity and crimes associated with this behaviour followed me for years and sent me to prison.

Because God calls us to leave wrath and revenge to Him[14] I had to forgive my abusers if I was to be released from their guilt; I had to deal with my hatred of the men whose identities I'd scribbled down on my list. The Bible is clear: God makes us all accountable for our own reactions and attitudes to things that happen to us no matter how shocking. Jesus said that it was not what enters a man that makes him unclean, but what comes out of a man that defiles him, things like evil thoughts, sexual immorality, theft, murder, adultery, greed, malice, deceit, lewdness, envy, slander, arrogance, and folly. My feelings of shame made me hide what had occurred to me, but my own response to these men's actions led me to defile myself, and many others, through a lifetime acting out this litany of sin. My own reactions to my abuser's actions was the catalyst that propelled a perversity that always sought pleasure but never found satisfaction.

For many years loneliness and isolation dwelt with me. I purposely isolated myself from my family, my culture and my place of origin. Extreme loneliness eventually became the root of much evil in me, it caused me to seek out like-minded people. The book of Proverbs says a man who isolates himself is an angry man.[15] I saw how the more isolated and lonely I became the more rage built up inside me. It was anger I learned to hide, rage I had no answer for and an explosive fury I had no way of containing. Add alcohol to the mix and you had a ticking time bomb. Alcohol became a sealing agent for entry into the gang environment. I used to drink with all the brothers whose lives were similar to mine - it felt comfortable, we were unified in comradeship and it seemed I finally belonged somewhere. Very quickly I had drifted into the gang world.

Every scripture I read or heard spoke volumes about me, and the situations I found myself involved in. Some of those words were:

'Do not get drunk on wine, as it leads to debauchery'.[16]

It was so accurate. Alcohol led me directly into a world of debauchery, a world I came to treasure and love, a world with no boundaries. Accepting and reacting to sexual abuse, the effects of isolation and loneliness, stoking the fire of anger, drunkenness and debauchery were all added to the list of sins I had compiled that night.

Idolatry was also spoken about in the lectures. I listed it as a sin I was guilty of. I had never even heard the word idolatry until attending this school, I had no idea what it meant, but it became something I realised to be a giant stronghold over my life. The first of the 'ten commandments' says:

'You shall have no other gods before me.'[17]

Anything in my life I had made more important than God was an idol. Ignorantly I allowed my anger, my sexual desires, and my loneliness to become idols in my life. They influenced every decision I made. However, perhaps the greatest idol to rule my life was the image of the dog, the mongrel I wore on my back. My allegiance to the simple drawn image of the bulldog was total. I identified with the dog; I called myself a dog; I greeted my brothers as dogs ('Seig Heil Doggy'); I spoke dog language; I was as fierce and territorial as a dog; I fought like a dog; I wore the dog on my back as a patch and as a permanent tattoo. I was fully Mongrel. My body is covered with the dog insignias of the various chapters I associated with. The dog took many different forms, the angry dog, the dog with a spiked collar, the dog with a German helmet, the dog with a bone in its mouth, the dog in profile, the fierce dog, the full frontal dog, I bowed down to everything that was the dog and I made him my god - the mighty bulldog in the sky.

Without even knowing it I had worshipped the dog in every anti-society action I committed, religiously dedicated as I was to this animal. I became a dog in every way, he was my idol, the thing I lived for, and I placed the dog above everything else in my life. The funny thing was I hated dogs, always have. I've never even possessed a dog as a pet yet I took on the image of the dog, I loved and trusted it for life. When I heard the saying, 'Whatever thy heart clings to and relies upon, that is properly thy God,' I realised this was true of me and the dog was imprinted on my heart. The book of Romans explains how when a man exchanges the glory of God for an image of immortal man, birds, animals or reptiles, he is given over to the sinful desires of his heart and especially to sexual impurity.[18] These words were so true to my own nature. I pondered how the simple drawn image of a dog became an image for my worship, which led me into perverse sexual behaviour and the degradation not only of myself but many others. The truth of this can be seen in the symbol of the bulldog having sex with a woman often found tattooed on many of the

Mob guy's bodies. I was overcome by the image of that dog and what it stood for. It had a leash on me. While I believed it stood for brotherhood, comradeship and freedom, the dog also led me into corruption.[19] I know now that this sounds glib but living with God is the total opposite of living with the dog. We used to say the dog was god, yet the names 'dog' and 'god' are different ends of one spectrum in image and in nature. Ignorantly I had replaced immortal God with a canine imposter I idolised for nearly half my life. Embracing the dog gave me the freedom to combat loneliness with drugs, booze, violence and sex, or so I thought. It turned out to be a mirage.

The seriousness of sexual sin in my life did not truly hit me until after an incident that brought the full reality of it into full frontal focus. During a community excursion associated with the school I met a beautiful local woman I greatly desired. Without any sexual activity for a long period of time that part of me was screaming for release - I just wanted to get my rocks off. I gave into my old nature and like the predator I was, I found myself in a sexual embrace with this beautiful woman. After this night of passion a heavy burden of guilt came upon me, something I had never felt before.

Because the Bible speaks of sexual immorality as a sin against a man's own body, the same body Jesus regarded as a temple where God dwells,[20] it brings death to the body and causes the temple to become void of God who cannot dwell where sin is. When my conscience woke to this fact I came before my leaders and confessed my actions, repented to God and asked forgiveness of the woman for leading her into this situation. I was stepped down from any further excursions but given the option to continue with my studies. This affair exposed the full nature of my whole previous sexual lifestyle, which was linked to misogyny or my ill-treatment of women. An arm tattoo of a woman in bondage, a woman with a snake between her legs, and a skull surrounded with dead women is a reminder of my old gang thinking about sexuality and women.

The gang world was the perfect place for me to foster my own sexual predatory nature, passed onto me by my original abusers; I was free to pursue my compulsion for satisfaction. However, I was never really fulfilled and it actually left me lonelier than ever before. That loneliness increased my appetite for union in the form of debauchery, wrong unity and flagrant sexuality. The image of the dog sexualising a woman was the image that represented who I was then and I didn't know what it was to protect and love our women. Whatever form of lust passed through my mind I fed through immoral sex, while rage and anger controlled the treatment I handed out to women.

The shame, guilt and the reality of the hurt became overwhelming - I was brought to my knees groaning and wailing with tears that night. I'd defiled everyone I had touched including myself. I knew I had to repent and seek forgiveness from God as well as from those I had hurt, something I knew could take a lifetime. These parts of my past I penned on the page.

Jesus speaks of many who will be offended, betray and hate.[21] There is a progression here of the road to anger, hatred, violence and lawlessness. I was abused and deeply compromised and that sense of betrayal and anger in me spawned hatred - that is being 'void of love'. I was completely 'void of love' for anyone, I didn't know how to love, love was getting the bash. Jesus speaks about how those who have been emotionally hurt will harbour an offence or grudge and react with anger and hatred. Those who harbour these emotions are easily deceived by false prophets and enticed into worlds that feed that hatred. Eventually they isolate themselves and become a law unto themselves, and led by this lawlessness they seethe with anger. This is a perfect description of how I was in the Mob. We were all offended in some form or another, abused by people in our families, by strangers, or simply offended by the system. Deep in our hearts we felt betrayed and we were filled with hatred, which revealed itself in the form of murder, rape, suspicion, and rage. Lawlessness ruled amongst us, we never denied it but we lived it to the hilt. Hate, violence, anger, revenge and fighting were my lot. I loved it, I lived it, I breathed it, I fostered it and I earned the nickname 'Bruising Bruno' because that lifestyle became as intimate and as all-encompassing as the skin that covered me. The attitude of utu or revenge against an enemy was central to that hatred and lawlessness.

I still had thoughts, even at Bible school, about utu and wanting to kill people who I deemed were against me. Such are the tentacles of Mobsterism. I even felt this way toward some of my fellow students who I felt didn't understand me. Many times I had to ask the forgiveness of the people I hated at the school to the extent that it began to seem like a daily repentance. I even wanted utu against my old Mongrel Mob mates who I blamed for taking my leadership away and forcing me to become a loser. As I planned revenge, other Mobsters toyed with utu against me: They wanted me dead, make no bones about that. For my own part, I knew where my enemies slept, how drunk they could get, and everything about their whereabouts; I knew exactly where to attack the beating heart of those guys if that was what I really wanted. However, I never carried out my crazed plans because I submitted to a Christ consciousness that asks each of us to love our enemies, to do good to them and to bless them. In other words I embraced the golden rule: to do unto others that which I would have them do unto me.[22] But I was under no illusion that I was in a battle of competing forces and there were times when deep down I thought I didn't want to relinquish my right to utu. To defeat that, I had to become nothing before God and forge a new mind. I believe the Greeks called it metanoia (change your mind or repent). Holding tight to the precepts of Jesus I never put my utu plans into action. Jesus never sought revenge for his humiliations. So what did I, a corrupted mortal, really have to complain about? I submitted to Jesus' words to love my enemies because He did.

These were some of the attitudes, beliefs, thoughts and actions I lived by and recognised as my sin. By writing them down I had finally admitted openly what and who I was. I recognised I had chosen the life I led and I was responsible for all my decisions, no-one else. I laid my list of crimes and misdemeanors, my ideas and sins before God and considered what I was to do next.

The next morning I interrupted a class and explained to the lecturer and my fellow students how I had been woken by the Holy Spirit in the middle of the night and told to write down all my sins. I knew I had to openly confess them before my new brothers and sisters, people I trusted would not judge or criticise me, people I knew who were in the same boat, people who like me also had to give an account of themselves to each other and to God so that forgiveness and healing could occur. As an encouragement I was reminded of the scripture in John 1:9 that says:

> *'If we confess our sins He is faithful and just to forgive us*
> *and to cleanse us from all unrighteousness.'*

I wanted to be forgiven and to feel clean. I felt so vulnerable and this was a feeling I had always considered a weakness and I hardened myself against it. It was a feeling I had never experienced before, I had to strip myself of self to stand before everyone and read aloud this huge list of crimes against God, against humanity and against myself.

I confessed before them all, repented and asked forgiveness for my actions. Knowing that God had forgiven me because of my confession and my public act of repentance, I was embraced by my brothers and sisters with open arms. It was probably the first time I had felt the touch of genuine love for many years. It was a heart wrenching experience. I was told to burn my list of transgressions as a sign that God had placed them behind him never to remember them again. As we set the list alight the papers refused to burn. I was mortified and it was as if even God couldn't forgive me of my past. Three times the pages would not burn, the flames stopping on specific texts in the list - a sign perhaps that there were strong demons that resisted leaving me or that I was not truly willing to release to God. After the third try all the pages finally ignited and were consumed by the flames. Moments later they were completely reduced to ashes.

Considering my past in this manner was harsh, severe and sad, as well as cleansing, healing, enlightening, and very powerful. After this incident I would often find myself weeping, crying, and sobbing sometimes uncontrollably. I became totally vulnerable and weak for the first time in living memory. I would lock myself in seclusion and hide from people. I didn't want anyone around me. I felt I couldn't take people staring at me, it was like they could see right through me. I couldn't take their criticisms, judgements or harsh words. The realisation of my guilt became too hard to bare - I felt unworthy to be forgiven - yet I knew God had offered freedom and forgiveness to me. Over time my faith and belief in a God-given forgiveness released me from continuous blame. If forgiveness was unavailable to me, having finally stared coldly at my actions, I would have wallowed in a permanent state of captivity, unworthiness and condemnation. I would still be chained to a dog collar and locked in a cocoon of self-hatred to this day.

I compared my situation to that of Lazarus who was called back to life from the grave by Jesus.[23] With his resurrection from the burial cave he still needed his burial clothes to be unraveled, his death wounds to be tended, and his emotions comforted from his death experience. I was in that same position. I had become born again to the spirit of God through Christ and resurrected from the pit of death, but I had grave clothes still to be removed, wounds to be healed, and my emotions to be comforted by the love of men I could trust, who could disciple me and mentor me for life. This process still continues in my life today.

Receiving God's forgiveness does not mean I am totally absolved from my life. I am aware I am still at the mercy of the consequences of my actions. I still must reconcile with this world, and confront those I hurt when the opportunity presents itself. All I can do is ask forgiveness and lay myself at the mercy of those I have inflicted with pain. Whatever punishment they might want to vent on me I will take, and as long as I keep my heart right with God I'll make retribution for the past and serve them.

I knew at that point of my confession why Jesus Christ was crucified. He was a sin sacrifice for my crimes, he rose from the grave to defeat death and sin, the same death and sin my life was immersed in. By believing who he said he was, and receiving his forgiveness I was freed from the clutches of the sinful nature and made presentable to God. I also had free access to the law of the spirit to help me fight my battles and live a life of truth and joy. I wanted to live by the law of the spirit of God not the sinful nature of the dog. The fruit of the dog was death but the fruit of the spirit is love, joy, peace, patience, kindness, goodness, faithfulness, gentleness and self-control.[24] I wanted my life to represent these qualities.

It was not easy to accept this initially. My old self opposed those traits and I hated them, they just weren't me at all. I had to train my whole being to become them. By self-control I had to review every day of my life to ensure the sinful nature does not take hold. But the power of Christ to change a gangster like me is manifest.

Walking this new talk is a daily struggle and challenge for me, I keep God's word close to my heart and I try to live it to the letter to help me survive the days. I take solace in the following scripture from Proverbs 3:1-2:

> *'My son, do not forget my teaching, but keep my commands*
> *in your heart, for they will prolong your life many years*
> *and bring you prosperity'*

Chapter Thirteen
GOD RULES

Attending the annual Baptist Assembly hui while at the Bible school was always interesting. There were two occasions while attending these gatherings that had profound meaning for me. One of these incidents occurred at the 1993 Assembly hui on Auckland's North Shore. I stood on a stage with the leader of Pukekohe Black Power, pressed his nose to mine in a holy embrace, to publicly reconcile our differences as individuals and as members of opposing gangs. He had just recently joined the Bible school and as was the usual the students became helpers and servants for these functions. At a pre-ordained time the stage was opened for the students to perform or speak. This Black Power brother stood to voice the story of his past and his desire for reconciliation. I knew this guy and my memory took me back to a day ten years earlier when I had been on remand at Waikeria Prison. I made a pact with a Maori prisoner there who told me about his son who was in the Black Power. I told him then that he, his son and I, as a representative of the Mob, would always be brothers - a pact of peace and protection. The Black Power leader standing on the stage before me this day was that Maori guy's son. I took the opportunity to make a true reconciliation stance that day and present myself before this brother to lay to rest the rivalry of our personal gang pasts with a hongi, our noses pressed hard together in the Maori way, our eyes meeting face to face, and our hands in each other's embrace. This was to be a significant moment for both of us. We truly were spiritual brothers at that very moment.

A similar incident occurred at a 1996 international cultural gathering of the Baptist Assembly in Rotoiti where cultures from all around the world were represented. On the last evening, set aside as a cultural expression night, I was led to walk across the stage and reconcile with a long serving Pakeha judge. We shook hands, performed a hongi and embraced each other as brothers in the Lord - a gang member representing lawlessness and a judge representing the law. There was no dialogue. It was a vital moment, a visible demonstration of sincere reconciliation through Christ that made background, race and creed pale into irrelevancy. You could have heard a pin drop; there wasn't a dry eye in the place; I had finally made my peace with the law in a meaningful way. All my weapons of destruction against the legal system were laid down and buried from that day on - the power and necessity of reconciliation was firmly imprinted on my heart.

Expressions of reconciliation like this are aspects of true Christianity that deeply interest me. Having lived the life I did I am constantly confronted with situations where I am humbled to express reconciliation due to my past. I am not daunted in going down that track. Reconciliation should follow a path of confessing to the hurt, and to the victims. Repentance should be followed by meaningful action that forges reconciliation with previous enemies or victims. For many reconciliation is seen as a 'cop out' if it doesn't incorporate some sort of restitution or payment. According to biblical reconciliation processes restitution and restoration is essential. This is the power, within your means, to restore what was destroyed or lost through the original act.

In 2005 I was contacted by the TV3's 60 Minutes programme to participate in a live interview with a woman who was viciously raped by Mongrel Mob gang members in the 1980s after shopping in Taumarunui. I knew I was not part of this particular incident but I felt I could offer some form of reconciliation to this woman. She told me her story and in the spirit of honest enquiry asked me why the Mob felt they had to do such an act. I could give her no real answer except to bluntly say: 'That's what they do.' At the meeting I apologised to her on behalf of the Mob and asked her forgiveness. She accepted my expression of repentance on behalf of the Mongrel Mob even though my guilt only stretched to my association with the Mob not to the physical act itself. I stood in the gap that day not for my own sake but for the sake of a woman who wanted some form of resolution to allow her to move on with her life.

At the time of this incident I had just submitted a compensation claim to the courts for the period I spent in jail for wrongful imprisonment. I felt I was entitled to some form of restitution. I was initially suspicious that TV3's request on this occasion was a ploy by the system to discredit my compensation claim by pinning this woman's attack on me. However, after confronting this woman's need for closure and hearing the advice of my Christian mentors, I also had to close a chapter of my life by letting my compensation claim go, leaving restitution to God.

Back in October of 1997 I was part of a national Christian gang hui held in Pukekohe to offer spiritual assistance for those gang members who wanted something different but didn't know how to go about it. The hui was a forum to discuss ways to reach those brothers and sisters in the gangs, and those in jail with the message of Ihu Karaiti (Jesus Christ).[25] The conference also highlighted an awareness of the struggles those with similar backgrounds to me have when trying to live the Christian life within the church. There was a sense that the church and the gang members in Christ needed to unify and reconcile with each other. During the course of the weekend the leaders of the hui recognised the plight of abused women in the gangs by asking the men present to humble themselves and wash the feet of the women at the hui. Many women responded to the call and a number of ex-gang members bent down on their knees to wash the women's feet as an act of repentance for the way they as men in the gangs had treated women in general. I remembered how my mentors had humbled themselves to wash my own feet and now I too had to humble myself alongside other ex-gang brothers to wash the women's feet. It was a very emotional moment filled with tears and wailing - that to me is true reconciliation. I learned that day what being a real man was. That hui saw a testament of reconciliation between gang members and God, rival gangs, men and women, Pakeha and Maori, and gangs and the church.

I believe the process of reconciliation to be central to healing the rift between society and the individual members of the gang world. Reconciliation to me means working together to find ways to ensure life (not death) permeates the lives of those want to change. The true power of reconciliation will also become apparent when we apply its power to the young generation. As past and current gangsters reconcile with their at-risk sons, daughters and grandchildren will we see a stay in the growth of youth gang culture? Many of the current youth gangs are the children and grandchildren of old gangsters. Almost inevitably they will lead the same lives we did unless we become examples of the way new life should be lived. We as fathers need to ask forgiveness of our own fathers or whoever, whether dead or alive, for ill-treating us. Without this we will never turn back the inter-generational tide. We need to repent of our own heinous actions, disrespect and ill-treatment toward our own children and families. If we turn our backs on this we will be guilty of allowing our own iniquity - hatred, violence, sexual perversion, misogyny and anti-societal values - to pass through our children to other generations. Because we have made the iniquity of the dog an idol in our lives, absorbed his psyche and worshipped him in our actions, God must judge our sin 'punishing the children for the sins of their fathers to the third and fourth generation.'[26] As harsh as this may sound we ourselves have heaped this legacy on our descendants by acting the way we have in our past. For the sake of our children, grandchildren and great-grandchildren we must put right our own actions, heal old wounds and turn from ways that simply lead to death both literally and figuratively. In saying this the same scripture also says God will 'bless a thousand generations of those who love him and keep his commandments.'[27] Is this not what we want for our children? Blessings not curses?

The current behaviour of at-risk youth searching for brotherhood and acceptance in gangs is no different to my journey. In many ways their lives are directly related to our actions and example. I don't believe we created safe family environments for our families; how could we, we didn't even respect them. The lack of respect our children have for us, who have abused them outright, could promote a generational cycle of violence and dysfunction. Our children are a lot more vulnerable today courtesy of some insidious influences - alcohol, methamphetamine, heroin, cocaine, internet pornography, blasphemy, misogynistic song lyrics and violent music - all of which sanction and fuel a sinful nature that ends up potently and aggressively controlling their lives. I see the young gangs today as different to my generation; they are more dangerous and violent and they feed like sharks - the smell of blood in their gills - off sophisticated and accessible temptations.

In the end I believe we must be watchful caring parents for our children, protective and gentle people who care about what our children are up to, making sure strangers and family members do not abuse them. If we as parents have destructive baggage in our backgrounds feeding our relationships with our children, these things will become a seed planted in our children that will invariably shape their lives. Violence breeds violence, bitterness breeds bitterness, and a lack of love breeds hatred. If you tie a dog to a tree and everyone who comes past it kicks it, when you release that dog he will bite anything in its path. Put simply, as responsible parents we need to deal with the past, put the offences, anger, rejections and hurt to one side and instill love in the hearts of our children and grandchildren.

Together with many of my gang brothers and sisters, I do not want to see our kids and grandchildren follow the path we did. It's taken me a lifetime, and only now do I feel I have the tools to be a parent to all my children. I ask forgiveness of my children and my family if my actions have ever hurt them and I release them to the hands of God. If we don't do this as men, we will perish like many of my brothers have. But none of this can be accomplished without knowledge of God. The prophet

Jeremaiah wrote:

> *'...For I know the plans I have for you declares the Lord,*
> *plans to prosper you and not to harm you, plans to give*
> *you hope and a future. Then you will call upon me and*
> *come and pray to me and I will listen to you. You will*
> *seek me and find me when you seek me with all your*
> *heart and I will be found by you and bring you back from*
> *captivity ...'*[28]

Do we not want a future and hope for our children? I do! Most of my life I had no concept of a future or even an inkling of the hope for a future. Now that I have something of it in my spirit, in my heart and running through my veins nothing can separate me from that. I want this for my children, I want their dreams to become a reality. We need to responsibly prepare our children for the realities of life that includes teaching them the values and promises of God. No doubt they will lead their own lives but if we do right by the family, they will return to us in time. Crucial to this process is the need to love them unconditionally irrespective of their struggles in life.

The Bible story of Joseph that Porky's father relayed to me many years ago, still echoes in my mind and many parts of that story I can identify with. Joseph was innocently thrown into prison for the accusation of sexual immorality, just as I was accused and convicted for sexual crimes I was innocent of. He too was imprisoned but resurrected to life to become one of the rulers of Egypt allowing him to bring his whanau to the riches of a new life. This is now where my heart lies and as an ex-gang member it is my mission to speak wisdom to others from my background, young and old, about the change and transformation that can bring them new life.

I know God has saved me from abuse, drowning, car accidents, attempted assassinations, drunk driving and numerous near death experiences for a greater purpose than to simply rot in jail or be deposited in an early grave. My life is now about bringing true change to gang families to heal their wounds and help restore their lives. And I work on the principle that it's possible to unleash the collar of the dog so a new ethic can be imprinted on their hearts.

Having separated myself from the Mob for a time, realigning myself to a spiritual perspective on life, I knew I would one day have to return to my old world as a changed person and as a witness to the work of Christ in me. That day came when I was asked by a Christian lady who supported our ministry to attend the funeral of a Mobster I knew who had died a violent death. I found it hard to say 'yes' as I believed I was now too divorced from the dog culture. It wasn't an easy decision and I was full of fear about how the brothers would take me. Nevertheless, I agreed to go as an ambassador for Christ. This is where the rubber meets the road; this is what I was called to do. But this time I attended a tangi wearing a different patch, a Christian patch. Dressed in red I went amongst them in all humility, I was there to support the kaupapa of the day with a loving heart for the deceased and his whanau. Many of the guys acknowledged my presence but found it very hard to relate to me or even know how to talk to me anymore. I had changed so much that they found communication hard - I didn't have that dog persona or dog speak on my tongue any more. But crucially, they did not disrespect me.

Since that time I have had many nights where I have been woken up by the Holy Spirit and compelled to pray on my knees for the Mongrel Mob without really knowing why. Without fail I would wake-up the next morning to hear of the death of a brother in the gang. I know my life is intertwined with the gangs but it is a link that differs from before. It is now about intercession - prayer and the battle for their lives. I don't want the guys who have lived the life I did to live and die in violence, in an immersion that is without hope.

I remember hearing about a Mob brother from the King Country, an associate of mine over many years, who was dying and needing compassionate leave to be released from prison so that he could live out the rest of his life in the care of his family. Everyone knew him as Pup. I'd first met him when I was told to go and pick him up from Rangipo Prison. He was only seventeen at the time, but already a seasoned felon from regular time spent in 'boys homes'. He was a caring-natured brother who was attracted to the comradeship of the gangs and he joined the King Country chapter. Pup had to prove himself as a prospect to be patched, but eventually another brother vouched for him and spoke of his prison term. He had an X-factor which, combined with a staunch nature, endeared him to the whole chapter. To be accurate, he was fearless. It was no problem for him to pull a gun on the cops. I personally loved Pup for many reasons - he always looked after my back - despite the fact that some of his actions had caused mayhem in my own life. His life had been marred by continually being sent to prison.

However in this situation he had cancer and was coming to the end of his days. As soon as I heard about his illness, I immediately went to visit him in the North Shore Hospital but first I asked well-known Christian evangelist Bill Subritzky to accompany me. Bill didn't hesitate and Pup, festooned with tattoos, was grateful to see us. I introduced him to Bill as a minister of the Bible. Pup knew the Bible but because he lived in the Mob he kept it very quiet. He was the one in prison with me years earlier who'd seen me try to hide the Bible I had received from my sister. Bill prayed for him and intuitively knew through the Holy Spirit that he had been removed from his family by the age of seven and this had set the course for the rest of his life. I saw the tears begin to well up in Pup's eyes, embedded amidst his heavy facial tattoos and rough exterior. As we prayed together Pup recited the prayer of salvation and surrendered his life to Jesus. Bill saw a huge warrior angel standing behind him as a protector to reaffirm his life. In the coming days the wall in his hospital room was covered in positive stuff. He was finally granted his compassionate release from prison after the nurse in the 'Parry Maxi' hospital agreed that he no longer posed a threat to society (5 months prior to his death). Following his release, Pup began a journey to try and make peace with people especially the brothers, including me over some of his past actions. During this time I traveled overseas. One night my spirit was so restless I could not sleep. I prayed that evening until the restlessness in me subsided. That same evening I received a vision of Pup with short hair, at peace with God. I knew then he had passed on. For me, the haircut was a symbol that Pup's heart had been fully surrendered to God. You may ask why would God be interested in bad-ass gangsters like us? Why would He allow guys like Pup and I the privilege of mercy, love, restoration or access to a Heaven, after all crime and evil that has clung to us like a beggar's rags? I mean, let's face it, that's not fair! Why should I shelter under the same tree as other more righteous citizens of this world? In my mind the answer is simply:

'For God so loved the 'world' (people like us) that he gave

his one and only Son, that whoever believes in him shall
not perish but have eternal life.'[29]

Jesus died on the cross between two criminals; one of them believed who he was and one did not. Jesus came to the world for the unloved, the poor, beggars, prostitutes, prisoners and murderers to show them a way to be released from bondage and captivity. While the 'world' may never release or forgive us of our crimes God will forgive us and restore us if we just believe in his work and genuinely turn from our 'wicked ways.' After all, his son 'took the rap' for people like us.

My life is now concerned with seeing true change take place amongst the gang community who want to have their wounds and families healed, the leash of the dog released from their necks and a new ethic or foundation for life imprinted on their hearts. A life not dictated by the dog but ruled by God.

True Red

EPILOGUE

I received the following letter recently. The writer's words and her personal story I thought would make an appropriate epilogue or conclusion for this book. An edited version of this letter is presented here in its original form. Receiving this letter has greatly encouraged me to continue the journey I presently walk; it has given my personal path in life true meaning. If my testimony is able to change one person's life for the better then my own life has not been in vain. There is nothing else to say.

24 July, 2007

Kia Ora Tuhoe

Words cannot express how grateful I am to you for sowing those wonderful, hopeful seeds from God, when I first meet you, over six years ago. As you know, at the time, I was in a very violent relationship with an ex-Mongrel Mob member when you travelled down to Patea, to share your testimony at a church there. A friend had invited me to come along and if it wasn't for the fact that I was curious about how God could turn an ex-Mongrel Mob man (you) into a practicing Christian I would never have walked through those doors. Your testimony was truly amazing and I knew in my heart then that God had to be real to change your life so much. It was that very first night I heard you speak that I gave my life to Jesus.

My partner (at that time) was in jail and so following Jesus was going along great at first. He came out 3 months later and, of course, my life turned instantly back to crap. The physical, mental and verbal abuse picked up where it had left off. My life was once again in misery but I had a taste of what life was like with Jesus in it - I now knew there was more to life than what I was experiencing. That short time of my life with Jesus was the best I've ever felt. I ran away from him (like I always did). You and a lovely lady took me in and tried to help my baby and get our lives back on track. I will never forget the love and support you both showed me at that time of need and it was a lasting memory that I will always cherished. You showed me God's love first-hand.

My ex's influence and control on my life, coupled with the fear and loyalty I felt towards him, ended up pulling me back into an accustomed life of destruction. I spent the next two years trying to get out of the dark hole I had once again dug for myself but not having a clue on how to do it. What I did know now though, was that there was a God. It saved me Tuhoe!

I am now living in Nelson and have been a practicing Christian for four years. God has planted me in the church, under great leadership and my children and I are flourishing in every area of our lives.

God helped me free myself from that life of destruction for GOOD! He rose me up out of the ashes and helped me stand fast in HIS name. I do have my trials and tribulations at times, as God continues to clean me up on the inside but nothing can compare to the pain I once endured before having a relationship with Him. I am NEVER going back to where I've come from - not EVER! Life is fantastic now!

I have to let you know that the seeds you sowed six long years ago in my life have now germinated and grown. May you and those around you be encouraged, keep on keeping on and fighting the good fight for Jesus....He is using you mightily. God bless you for following your heart and being obedient to our God. If you hadn't of done that - I would not be here today and my children wouldn't have their mum! Now I have a testimony to share, too. The ripple effect of all of this Tuhoe, is that my younger sister now serves the Lord because of what He has done in my life. She couldn't believe how much I had changed, how I was no longer in an abusive relationship and how good a life I was living now.

So, Tuhoe my brother...thank you so very very much. My little family and I are very grateful to the godly love you showed us all those years ago..With our God nothing is a coincidence. I love my life with Jesus. I will sign off here Tuhoe but you take care,OK. God bless you heaps! Bye.

Kindest regards,
...Sister..

END NOTES

1   New Zealand Herald, January 9, 1976, 'Unlikely Mob will Change'.
2   New Zealand Herald, January 8, 1976.'Minister's Plea at Funeral'
3   'Sour Grapes at Ambury Farm Park', The Listener, August 1, 1987.
4   NZ Herald, Auckland, Dec 13, 1986.
5   Ibid, 1986.
6   The Listener, August 1, 1987, p.28.
7   Luke 6:45.
8   Mathew 5.43-44.
9   John 1:42.
10   Genesis 3, Romans 5:12-21.
11   Romans 7:14.
12   Galatians 5:19.
13   Galatians 6: 8.
14   Romans 12:19.
15   Proverbs 18:1.
16   Ephesians 5:18.
17   Exodus 20:3.
18   Romans 1: 22-25.
19   2 Peter 2:19:'...promising them freedom by which they themselves are slaves to corruption; for by what a man is overcome, by this he is enslaved.'
20   1 Corinthians 6: 18.
21   Mathew 24:10-11.
22   Luke 6:26-31.
23   John 11:44.
24   Galatians 5:22.
25   'From Radical Mobster to Radical Christian', Franklin County News, October 21, 1997, p. A7.
26   Exodus 20:4-6.
27   Exodus 20: 4-6.
28   Jeremaiah 29:11-14.
29   John 3:16

True Red